CONˊ

CUO1507129

LESSONS FROM
ANTIOCH

LESSONS FROM
ANTIOCH

Exploring a biblical guide for
the contemporary church

SECOND EDITION

FREDDY HEDLEY

emblembooks

www.emblembooks.co.uk

This second edition published in Great Britain 2010
First published 2007

Unless otherwise indicated, biblical quotations are taken from the New International Version (NIV) © 1973, 1978, 1984 by the International Bible Society.

ISBN 978-0-9559594-3-1

Cover photo by Chris Rycroft. Design by MPH.

Edited and published by Emblem Books, Swaffham, UK
www.emblembooks.co.uk

For Ali

- i -

ACKNOWLEDGEMENTS

This book began as a time of sabbatical and study in May 2005, when I found myself at the end of a season of teaching in secondary schools and before joining the *Anglican Church Planting Initiatives* team. My study took me through the life of Barnabas and as I read, prayed and processed how I was challenged, many of the observations and principles that are outlined here emerged.

Since then these have been adapted, honed and added to through a mixture of personal experience and the wisdom of others. Many of these principles have proved invaluable as they have been learned and applied through my roles in church leadership, as well as in training and consultations for church planters or those involved in fresh expressions of church.

However, it is particularly the wisdom of others that have informed so much of the content of this book that I want to acknowledge. And right at the top of this list of amazing people must come Bob & Mary Hopkins.

Bob & Mary are the leaders of *Anglican Church Planting Initiatives* and have worked at the forefront of church planting and pioneering mission for over twenty years. It has been a tremendous privilege to work with them and every day continues to be a revelation, learning from their extensive knowledge and experience. They have contributed massively to the content and heart of this book, and there is no over-estimating the importance of their contribution to this book being published.

The chapter on how Antioch relates to church planting is directly taken from training material that Bob & Mary have developed over the last decade.

Acknowledgements

In addition I would like to acknowledge the input and encouragement of Tom Lawrie and Paul Lewis, both as friends and co-leaders of *Covenant Network Church*. They have inputted to the understanding and assurance of the principles laid out in this book more than they will realize and continue to be the pioneering heart behind so much of what I have learned thus far in church leadership and discipleship.

Throughout this book I refer to a number of different sources that have influenced me, but other than the content that has come through *Anglican Church Planting Initiatives* the biggest influence has come through the LifeShapes discipleship material that has been created and developed by Mike Breen. This forms a major part of the life teaching that has come through St Thomas' Church in Sheffield, where I am based, and has been a transforming factor in my life with Christ.

The LifeShapes material is used widely throughout this book, and is done so with sincere thanks to Mike for his permission to use it.

As well as Mike's teaching, which can be found in his books *The Passionate Church* and *A Passionate Life*, the principles of LifeShapes have grounded themselves in my life and experience thanks to the discipling relationships I have developed with Paul Maconochie and John & Liz Lovell. Again, the application of LifeShapes in this book would not have been possible without them.

Finally, I must acknowledge the love, support and contribution that has come from Ali, my wife, who has been such a vital factor in every aspect of our combined ministry and my understanding of growing as a Christian; and also my daughter Maisie, who brings so much joy through her smile!

And all this in the love and encouragement of Christ, without whom it would not have been worth picking up a pen in the first place.

FH, October 2007

- ii -

NOTES ON THE SECOND EDITION

This second edition of Lessons from Antioch has been written in the autumn of 2010, three years after the completion of the original text. In the intervening years I revisited the content of this book several times, both as I taught it and as I continued to be challenged to learn new things about the church in Antioch and what it can teach us today, and I realised there was more to say on the subject.

For the most part, the writing of this second edition has involved working through the existing text and adding further detail, more references and new observations to what was already asserted. However, the more I revisited the content, the more obvious it became that I had left one glaring omission first time around that had to be addressed: the importance of what the pioneer/apostle/missionary brings of him or herself to any Kingdom initiative, and in particular, the essential need for encouragement, as demonstrated in the life and ministry of Barnabas. Therefore, I have written a whole new chapter – What the Pioneer Brings (chapter nine) – which covers this in detail.

I am also extremely grateful to my friend and vicar Stephen Mawditt, leader of the Fountain of Life network in Norfolk, for his valuable input and editorial comments throughout this book, which have helped further shape my thinking and the way I present it.

The result is an additional 96 pages of updates, amendments, enhancements and new material. I sincerely hope and pray that this new edition builds on the foundations of the original and is genuinely inspirational, challenging and helpful for you in your context. And, of course, that you enjoy the read!

FH, September 2010

HOW TO USE THIS BOOK

This book can be used on two levels. Firstly you could just read it through and hopefully you will be blessed and challenged by some of the observations and principles that are written here. In which case how to read this book is perfectly simple, and can be approached in three phases - 1. Start at the beginning; 2. Make your way to the middle; 3. Read to the end.

Or secondly, you could use this as a practical workbook. At the end of each chapter there are questions to consider that have been written to help you go on a process of exploration, looking at your church context and unearthing potential ways forward in the context that Jesus has called you into. After each question there is given space for you to write your answers.

In addition, this book has been deliberately published with space between each line and wide margins to give plenty of room for taking notes. In short, this book is written to be written over. Add notes where you are challenged, cross out what you disagree with, scribble cross references or Scriptures I neglected to mention to your heart's content, so long as it helps focus your mind to what God may be saying and to learn how these principles best apply to you.

This could be done individually or as a group/team depending on your situation.

Either way, I hope this book proves to be a useful, informative, transformative, enjoyable read!

LESSONS FROM
ANTIOCH

LESSONS FROM ANTIOCH

1

THREE MODES OF CHURCH

The New Testament is essentially a blueprint for the church. Really, is that all?! Isn't it so much more than that? Well, it depends on how you see the church. If the church is, as the bible depicts, the people of God living their lives together for Jesus, then it is in the New Testament that we are given the detailed vision of what this should look like.

It begins, of course, with relationship. The church is all about relating to God the Father, Jesus the Son and the Holy Spirit, and what else are the Gospels about if not to guide us into entering this heavenly relationship with our eyes open and our hearts healed? If we don't have the relationship with Jesus, then our relationship with one another is less assured, less powerful, even less legitimate. But this is not a book primarily about relationship. For us to be able to cover what we need to in the short space we have, we need to take relationship as a given. None of what follows will work or make sense or be worth it without a community that has at its heart the desire for a living and impacting relationship with God.

After relationship comes lifestyle, based on the values of a transformed heart. How we live our daily lives for God as individuals and when we gather, is as much a mark of the church as who it exists for and what its formal practices look like. Loving one another, forgiveness, sacrifice, generosity, mercy, humility, all these are fundamental values and behaviours that make the church the church. And where do we learn how to live them out if not in the New Testament?

This is closer to what we want to look at in this book, but again this is primarily not a book about Christian lifestyle, which must again be an assumption.

20

This book is about how we address a strategy for bringing the relationship and lifestyle together to form a church community. And again, as we think of strategy it is the New Testament we must rely on. Within its pages we find a wealth of valuable detail about the circumstances that the early church was birthed into, throughout Jesus' ministry and in the aftermath of his death, not to mention the principles and practice of the movement of faith that followed in the power of the Holy Spirit.

Strategically thinking, this can especially be seen through the books of Acts and the Epistles, where we find the clearest biblical patterns and principles that shape how the people of God continue to gather today.

Over the years these have formed an effective manual for many new movements of the church, and have particularly influenced a major part of the theological base for the church planting movement over the last thirty years or so. They give a wide range of values and modes of church to work from, and are full of guidance and teaching for how to start, lead, grow and multiply a community of faith, through both the good and the difficult times.

The values and teaching are widespread and as you read through the Epistles particularly you get a sense of the heart of the Gospel being demonstrated differently in each place the church emerges, with priorities, practices and problems unique to each individual gathering of church from Jerusalem to Rome and everywhere in between.

So for example, the churches in the region of Galatia (those planted by Barnabas and Paul on their first missionary journey, Acts 13-14) had a particular problem with living a life not bound by the Jewish law. This largely Jewish collection of churches across Asia Minor and Europe had initially embraced the freedom that Christ offered, but some time after Barnabas and Paul left them another group of people came along (known as Judaisers) with the message that the Law was still fundamental for salvation. And in particular that, even though Gentiles now also had access to salvation, it could still only come through circumcision.

In response to this Paul writes his letter to the Galatians that communicates a Gospel of freedom: freedom from the Law, to live by the Spirit and serve God. The entire letter focuses on freedom, because Paul understands that this is the good news that needs to permeate the community of faith in this region, so that their values and priorities are founded on the liberty of Christ and can shape their behaviour and rituals.

But then we read through Paul's letters to the Corinthian church – written just six years or so later - and we read a different Gospel that he is describing, and different problems (and tailor-made solutions) he is highlighting. In Corinth conflicts had grown up within the church, between believers, over all sorts of issues.

So Paul writes his letters to them communicating the Gospel of unity and love. This extends to their unity in Jesus, their love for one another and the unity and love of marriage, as well as the recognition that their differences bring them together and make them more effective for the glory of the Kingdom, rather than drive them apart.

For the Corinthians, unity and love were the hallmarks of the Gospel that needed to be expressed.

Then in his letter to the Colossians, Paul implores them to live out a Gospel of submitting to Christ in all things in order to protect themselves from the threat of paganism that was creeping into their community.

In Thessalonica he taught them to live in the confidence of the resurrection, as their young faith was most vulnerable to their misunderstanding of what happened after death. Whereas, the letter to the Romans focused on the power of forgiveness, grace and faith over sin and temptation.

All through these letters there are clear examples of how these churches all had different issues, and how they needed to be encouraged to live out and have confidence in a different aspect of the Gospel unique to their circumstances. Paul's experience of travelling between these communities must have been one of seeing the same heart for Jesus expressed in so many different ways, as practices and priorities responded to the needs of the people and the aspects of the Gospel that most connected with them and enabled them to experience a powerful relationship with God.

However, if we search the New Testament for actual modes of the church, rather than the nature of the Gospel for particular situations, then the New Testament broadly gives us three … the church in Jerusalem, the church in Antioch and the churches planted by Barnabas and Paul across Asia Minor and Europe.

Diagram A (on page 29) shows both the spread of the New Testament church from Jesus to Rome, and the three modes of church that each stage of spread brought with it. For the purposes of communicating the difference between each of these levels of the New Testament church I have labelled them the Collected Church (Jerusalem), the Dispersed Church (Antioch, etc) and the Mobilized Church (Asia Minor).

Jerusalem is the Collected Church, because this is a unique time in the church's history when the whole of the church could be found in one condensed city. The entire world church was literally collected together in one place, and this had a massive impact on the experience and fruit of the church. There are miracles and blessings of every kind, inspired teaching, powerful prayer, amazing fellowship and courageous (and contagious) sharing of faith.

The famous "fellowship of the believers" passages of Acts 2:42-47 and Acts 4:32-35 are two such passages that show this in action, as well as the explosive growth that followed, and these have rightly become inspiring visions for what our fellowship should be like today.

However, in all honesty I often have found this a benchmark I can never reach, so that I read these passages and end up feeling disappointed at my inability to replicate what they did.

However, my disappointment stems from my having missed the point. It was an amazing, inspiring, transforming time but ultimately, a church in one place was not God's plan. The Gospel was not for Jerusalem alone – something Jesus had made clear with his final words in the company of his followers:

> *You will receive power when the Holy Spirit comes on you; and you will be my witnesses in Jerusalem, and in all Judea and Samaria, and to the ends of the earth.*
> **Acts 1:8**

In the end, something was always going to intervene and stop the church from becoming more about the place than the reason they started there. And so God, in His grace, allowed the church to be persecuted in order that it no longer be collected into one central mass but spread across the world so that more would be saved and His plan would progress apace.

And let us be in no doubt that such a persecution can include God's grace. Remember Jesus' affirmation:

> *Blessed are those who are persecuted because of righteousness, for theirs is the kingdom of heaven.*
> **Matthew 5:10**

Jesus understood how the love and power of God is called upon and released amidst persecution, how God's glory can shine and His kingdom can be advanced. Indeed, Jesus' words must have burned with clarity and encouragement as the Jerusalem Church experienced the very persecution he described.

They must have clung on to the promise that the kingdom was theirs so long as they held on to his love and freedom and didn't give in under the pressure of persecution. They must have discovered at first hand the truth that Paul later shed light on, that in our suffering God draws closer to us with the words:

My grace is sufficient for you, for my power is made perfect in weakness.
2 Corinthians 12:9

So in Acts 8 we see that this persecution of the church, which had existed from the first days, began to intensify to the point where the church was dispersed, hence the name of the second level.

Diagram A: The Spread of the New Testament Church

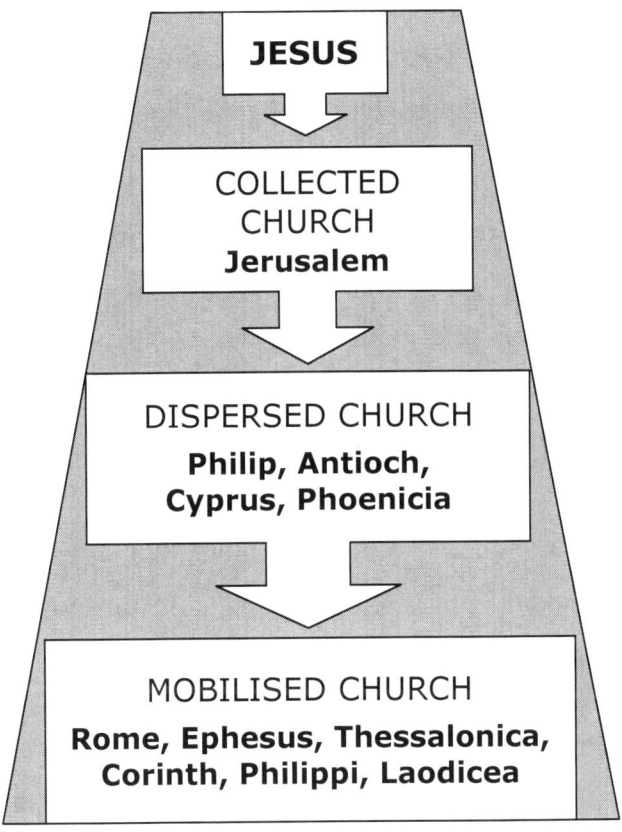

Once the church is dispersed we never quite see the fullness of the Acts 2 and 4 passages again, at least not recorded biblically. We do see much of the fruit emerging in different Christian communities, but in the same way that the church was no longer wholly collected, neither was the experience or the fruit. When you put it all together you do see the same things happening, but it is scattered (and therefore multiplied across a much wider area and to far more people). So for example there is an evangelistic focus for Philip, and a discipleship focus for Antioch.

This does not mean we should not pursue the full experience of the Collected Church. When they gather, we see all the features that collectively form the holistic church, which Jesus initiated so that we would all experience all of it as we live in community with him and one another.

When we look back at those early days we see a church defined by its place but we also see a church defined by its purpose. And it is this purpose that we continue to inherit today. Indeed, if we understand the implications of this properly then we can take a step back today and see that we still see all the same features in the Global Church today.

We may not see every New Testament miracle in our fellowship but if we are part of one Body of Christ then we are experiencing these miracles in our church, even more so now than two thousand years ago.

Having this perspective is an essential encouragement for us to pursue the same where we are, in the knowledge and expectation that the same fruit is available to us. But it should also protect us from being protected from discouragement when we don't see it happening in our front room, as we know that God is no less at work in us and in His church as a whole.

I have called the Asia Minor/Europe church plants the Mobilized Church because it is at this stage that we really see all the different aspects of the church at work in a networked, mobilized church – the result of the discipleship and connections of the wider church.

These three modes offer us a picture into how the first generation Christians approached different sizes of gathering, different mission contexts, different social challenges and alternative cultures. We will return to some of the specific observations we might make about the relationship between these three modes to one another in chapter three.

There is comfortably a book's worth of theology and understanding to be explored into how these modes juxtapose over the layers of society in the West today and what are the implications and challenges that the church, in its many forms and traditions, should perhaps listen to.

However, apart from occasional references to Jerusalem and Asia Minor/Europe to give us an understanding of the context, we will broadly concentrate our attention in this book on the church gathering in Antioch.

In particular, our main focus needs to be concentrated on what lessons we can learn that will enhance our understanding and experience of the contemporary church – be that in the more familiar, inherited mode of the local church, or be it church planting or fresh expressions of church.

As we explore how the church in Antioch started, as well as the challenges it faced, how it grew and thrived, through to how it became the greatest example of a church that releases missionaries and plants churches that we have in biblical record, we will look at how a church formed so long ago can continue to be a vitally relevant blueprint for us in today's culture.

We will also consider what lessons we can learn as we seek to develop the contemporary church, and the principles and values that we will need to guard at the heart of our mission if, like the Antioch church, we are to see the full fruit that Jesus has in store for our call as the church.

But let us begin by examining the context that the early Christians found themselves in when they first arrived in the city of Antioch.

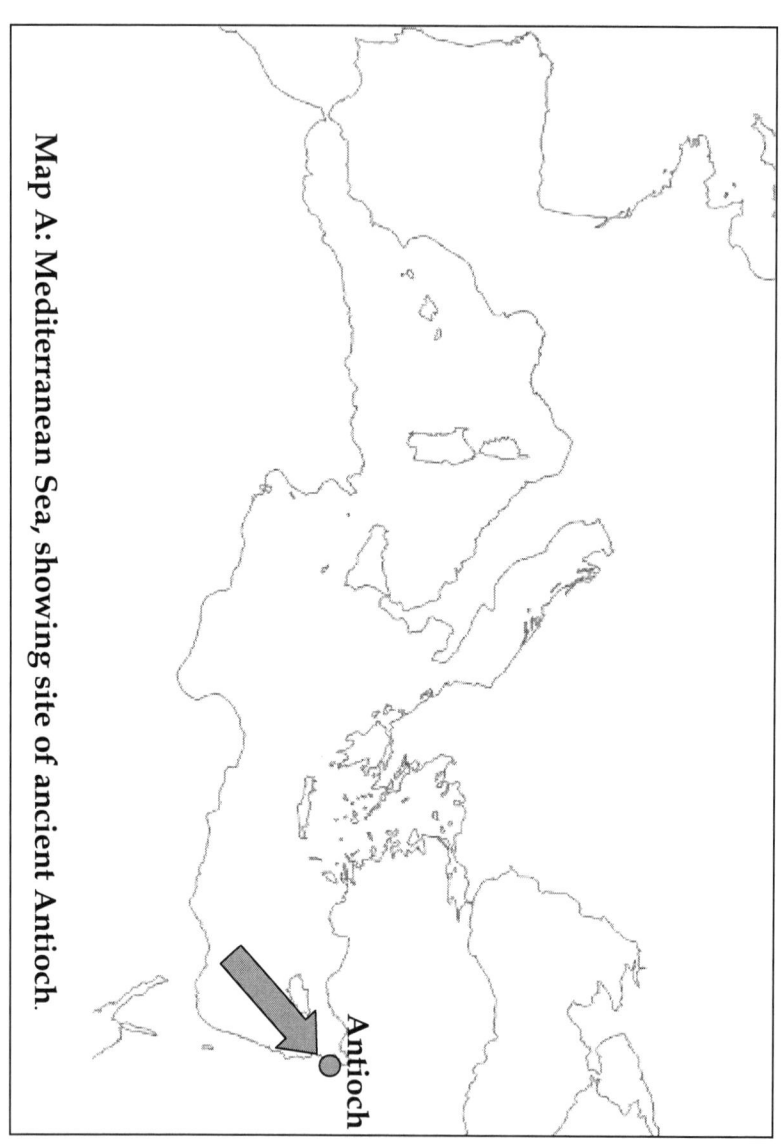

Map A: Mediterranean Sea, showing site of ancient Antioch.

Antioch

QUESTIONS TO CONSIDER

1. Does the church context you are called to most reflect the Collected Church, the Dispersed Church or the Mobilised Church?

Notes:

2. Is there a particular aspect of the Gospel that characterizes your church context?

Notes:

LESSONS FROM ANTIOCH

2

MISSION CONTEXT

The church in Antioch was planted in the wake of a great persecution that had broken out in Jerusalem (Acts 8:1). After the tensions surrounding Jesus' life and death among the religious and political authorities, it was hardly a surprise that the early church was a target for abuse, but it was so bad that after the stoning of Stephen (Acts 7:54-60) all the believers in Jesus (except, we are told, the apostles – the "sent ones"!) were forced to flee Jerusalem and scattered across Judea and Samaria, and beyond.

Persecutors such as Saul pursued the scattered church and sought to snuff out the rebellion from within the Jewish community. However, rather than discourage them from sharing the good news of Jesus this actually seemed to fuel them. We are told that, "those who had been scattered preached the word wherever they went" (Acts 8:4). Far from being quelled, the message of the resurrection was spread and the church grew.

After this a dramatic series of events began to unfold that would also have a profound impact on the future of the church. Philip took the Gospel into Samaria, Egypt and Caesarea (Acts 8: 4-40). Saul was converted (Acts 9:1-19). Peter had his vision and met with Cornelius, affirming that the Gospel was indeed for both Jew and Gentile (Acts 10:9-48).

SETTING THE STAGE

Each of these events played a significant part in the planting of the church in Antioch.

In Acts 11 we pick up the Antioch story. We read that as the church was scattered, people were sent as far as

Phoenicia, Cyprus and Antioch. In these places it was mainly to the Jews that the resurrection of Jesus was preached. At least it was for Phoenicia and Cyprus. In Antioch there was a group of Cypriots and men from Cyrene (in North Africa) who started preaching to Gentiles as well. The account tells us that "the Lord's hand was with them and a great number of people believed and turned to the Lord" (Acts 11:21).

Would this freedom to preach to the Gentiles have been possible if Philip had not broken the barriers by travelling first into the culturally remote Samaria and Egypt? Or if Peter, one of the leading apostles had not been given his revelation of a Gospel for all, which he in turn shared with the rest of the church?

The stories of what was happening in Antioch travelled far and such a level of blessing did not go unnoticed in Jerusalem. Barnabas was dispatched to see what was happening and to bring encouragement to the work of God. He in turn brought with him Saul and the two of them taught in Antioch and saw further growth and fruit.

But would this impact have been possible to the same degree if God had not prepared the way for Saul to first persecute the church in Jerusalem so that they were scattered as far as Antioch; and, if he had not then been converted himself to lead the movement to bring the message of Jesus to the Gentiles?

The birth of the church in Antioch was remarkable for the way that God had intervened to make it possible. And the fruit of the church in Antioch was to be that it grew and became an influential presence in the city community and in the wider church, not to mention in the spreading of Christianity as far as Rome.

Before we look further at how this was achieved, through faith and action, we must first consider what Antioch was like. What were those first Christians up against when they arrived in Antioch, and how relevant is their experience then to ours now?

ANTIOCH: AN OVERVIEW

The mission context for the Christians in Antioch was

remarkably comparable to the context the church finds itself in now in the West.

Antioch was a large, influential, bustling city in Syria (now southern Turkey). Behind Rome and Alexandria it was the third most significant political power-base in the Roman Empire, and of these three cities it was the least 'Roman', both in geography (in that it was the most remote from a condensed Roman stronghold) and in demographics (in that it contained more non-Roman communities to control than either Rome or Alexandria). It was to a greater degree a mixture of communities with Jewish, Greek, Roman, Arab, Syrian and Phoenician cultures all vying for their identity to mark the city.

However, there was never any doubt of it being a primarily Roman statement of power. The buildings were Roman, the rulers were Roman. It was overlooked by an Imperial Temple and the Roman citizens had their main meeting areas geographically sectioned off by the prominent Orontes river.

It was from this diverse and influential city that Rome would both rule and hold captive the 'risky' Jewish territories.

Its position near the Mediterranean and on the main landed trade routes between what is now Asia and Europe made Antioch a busy market city with a strong cultural focus on the importance of money. Social position and political power were also among the main ambitions of the people. Financially, it was the New York of its day.

In terms of modern day size, it was a city about the population of Sheffield (just over 500,000), but the spread of about the town of Rotherham (just under nine square kilometres). For anyone that knows these two neighbouring British conurbations, you will know that this makes for a very condensed, highly populated area. To add to this, large areas of the city were non-residential and so would have made the living conditions of the citizens even more crushed and stressful.

In the midst of this chaos there were many of the entertainments you would have expected from the best Roman cities, including theatres, a hippodrome, wide shopping streets, and many baths. An ancient West End!

The city itself had a highly urban culture, but on all sides it was surrounded by wide expanses of open country and farmland, sparsely inhabited by farmers and shepherds. With Antioch being a market city, this meant that the day-to-day mix of people would include regular traffic between the city and the country, with the rural edge of the city shaping the experience of the urban centre.

From archaeological research and exploration of the remains of Antioch, we can tell that within the city walls Antioch was built to be Roman in architecture, and was designed to hold a position of prominence in the area. The residents would have lived in a 'ghetto' culture, with each community having its own area of the city, separated by great outer and inner city walls and the prominent features of the city aqueduct and, most notably, the river Orontes.

These communities would come together in the everyday city centre busyness, but would return to their local indigenous roots at the end of the day, making Antioch a highly network-based city. Again, we can see this as a direct comparison to our modern day lives function.

The map on page 47 is a basic recreation of the ancient city put together from the current level of historical findings and research (as of 2007). It shows some of these features clearly, in particular the Jewish community sector, other residential areas (probably mainly Greek) and the very Roman city structure, with its colonnaded streets and the separate area containing the imperial palace and various Roman entertainments.

A PARALLEL FOR TODAY

In many ways Antioch was the centre of a culture very similar to the Western world today. Research of the available biblical, archaeological and literary evidence suggests that much like today it was a network-based, money and image focused society that was simultaneously affluent and poverty-stricken at its two extremes. It was a multi-cultural, multi-faith and multi-lingual, though still largely pagan community where many of the people were hard working, power hungry, status-centred, and politically aware.

This was a typically inner urban, highly pressured, sensually driven conglomeration of different peoples pressed together so tightly that their individual identities and values got lost at the expense of the overarching Roman machine. In the inner urban areas it would have been noisy, stressful and busy with people gathering primarily around work, entertainment and shopping… their homes being somewhere to escape to.

In the rural areas the home was the place of work, but the magnetism of the city necessitated regular trips in, forcing rural communities to be dependent on a culture that needed them, but still did not value them in return. For them their communities were their neighbouring farms, but these were spread so far and wide that they might not naturally mix unless given a central place to do so.

In both cases, Antioch was very like the culture and lifestyle of city life in the modern West.

And into this melting pot a group of scattered Jerusalem church planters, alongside some Cypriots and Cyreneans, found themselves driven to call together a church community that led to such impact on the city as to transform it forever, and saw some of the most prominent biblical missionary figures – such as Paul, Barnabas, Mark and Silas - raised up and sent out.

Map B: Ancient Antioch

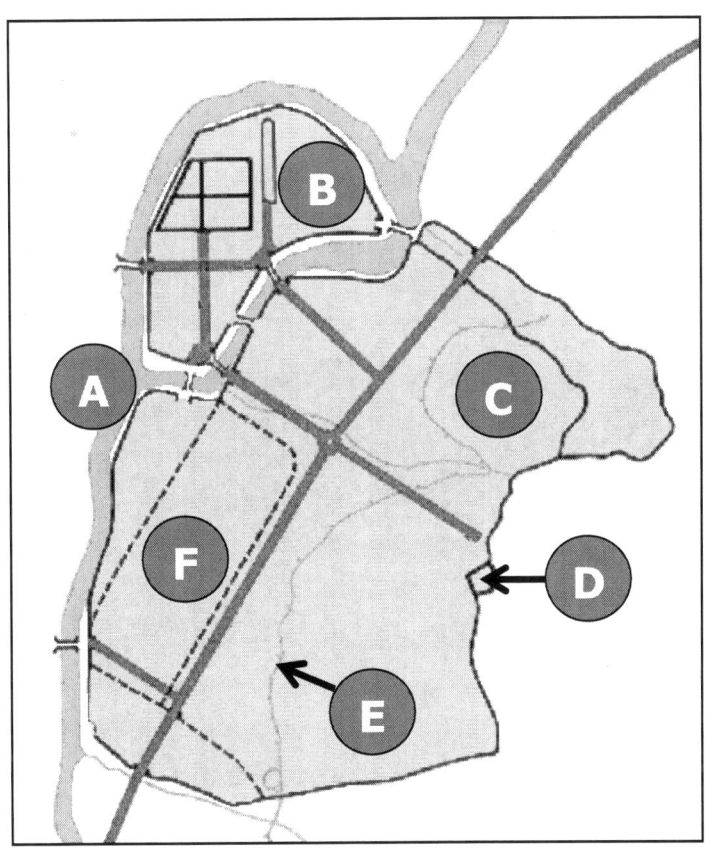

Key

A – River Orontes
B – Roman palace, bath, stadium, circus, etc
C – Residential area (Greek?)
D – Residential area
E – Aqueduct
F – Jewish community

QUESTIONS TO CONSIDER

1. What similarities can you spot between Antioch's context and yours?

Notes:

2. What ways can you already see to respond to this context?

Notes:

3. Begin to pray for God to give a vision for which aspects of your community to focus on.

Notes:

3

A BRIEF SUMMARY OF THE OTHER MODES

Although this book is broadly going to concentrate on the Dispersed Church mode of church to be found in Antioch, for us to properly understand how this related to the Collected and Mobilized Church modes (see *Diagram A*, page 29) it is necessary for us to have a basic overview knowledge of what these churches were like, so that when we refer to them we do so with a general understanding of the context and how they relate to the Antioch mode we are going to concentrate on.

Before looking at Jerusalem and Asia Minor, though,

it may prove helpful to briefly turn to a more contemporary observation of the church.

In their book, *The Shaping of Things to Come*, Alan Hirsch and Michael Frost highlight two broad forms of church from a mission perspective: Attractional Church and Emerging Church. In reviewing this more recently, Bob Hopkins has observed a third model – that of the Engaged Church.[1]

In its broadest terms, the Attractional Church bases its mission on the premise that the church must be a place that people can come to. Often this is expressed with seeker services, community events and church-based evangelistic courses (of which *The Alpha Course* is the most prominent example, though it is also true that Alpha is now increasingly being adapted into new presentational methods so that in different contexts it can equally apply to Attractional, Engaged and Emerging Church modes – indeed, there is a growing

---

[1] For a more in depth explanation of these models of church, Bob Hopkins' article *Making Sense of Emerging Church* can be downloaded from www.acpi.org.uk

movement of starting Alpha churches that emerge out of Alpha groups, often based in the home, which have taken the missional potential of Alpha into exciting new territory).

The Engaged Church is a body of people that first goes out, before bringing the people they engage with back to the church. The cell church movement has often given rise to good examples of this, as has the more recent cluster/mid-size congregation movement[2].

The Emerging Church is a body of people that goes out, engages with people where they are and allows church to emerge in that place, shaped by that culture.

This is the primary vision for the Fresh Expressions movement, which has already seen hundreds of new expressions of church emerge, big and small, in the few

---

[2] Phil Potter's book *The Challenge of Cell Church*, Bob Hopkins & Mike Breen's book *Clusters: Creative Mid-size Missional Communities* and Mark Stibbe and Andrew Williams' book *Breakout: One Church's Amazing Story of Growth Through Mission-Shaped Communities* are excellent exponents of the vision and strategies of both cell and cluster movements respectively.

years since the vision-casting *Mission-shaped Church* report in 2004.

There is no good or bad mode of church. These observations are not intended to imply one is more staid and inflexible, another more daring and contemporary. Rather it is better to think of the three modes as three community-shaped opportunities, depending on your mission context. Stephen Mawditt, vicar of the rural church plant Fountain of Life where I am based, has likened these three modes to different recipes for cooking a satisfying mission meal! The church community and the mission context are the starting ingredients, which are mixed together in fellowship and outreach by the Holy Spirit who also adds the heat and draws out the distinctive colour and flavour as he stirs it up.

The result is a vibrant expression of church, which is shaped by God in a particular way, at a particular time, for a particular context, and may very well be Attractional, Engaged or Emerging, according to what serves the community best.

Diagram B: The three shapes of the New Testament church

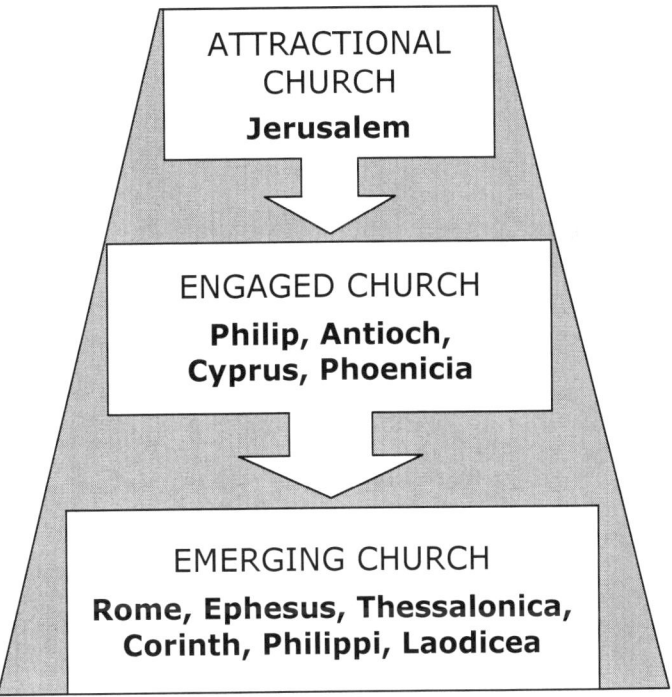

Let us consider how each of these three 'recipes' played themselves out in the account of the spread of the Gospel and the church throughout Acts:

THE ATTRACTIONAL RECIPE

The Church in Jerusalem from the time of Jesus' ascension until the church was scattered after the persecution is the biblical recipe for an Attractional Church. It shared all the same encouragements and challenges. It was the first mass gathering of Jesus' followers after the death and resurrection of Christ, and it gravitated into a central Jerusalem-based community led by the eleven remaining apostles.

Starting at Pentecost, it was a fast-growing network of believers that began with the Eleven and a handful of Jesus' other followers. But as a result of Peter's Pentecost sermon, the testimony of the believers, the evidence of miracles and the witness of the integrity of those that gathered in Jesus' name, the church grew rapidly to several thousand.

In modern day terminology, this first church was the centre of the first revival. Of course, it hadn't happened before … revival means "to become alive again"… so perhaps it was more of a vival!?

The book of Acts refers to three main ways that the church in Jerusalem witnessed and grew:

Firstly, it was through the testimony and preaching of the believers, and particularly the apostles. We see this in the accounts of Pentecost (Acts 2:1-41) and Stephen (Acts 7).

Secondly, it was the example of the Kingdom of God working in the lives of the believers, creating community and releasing the transformation of lives throughout Jerusalem. We see this in the two passages in Acts that describe how the church lived as a community (Acts 2:42-47 & Acts 4:32-35).

And thirdly, it was through demonstrations of the power of the Kingdom of God. For example, Peter healing the beggar at the Temple Gate (Acts 3:1-10).

It is also important to highlight that throughout each of these encounters there is a common thread of the Word of God being the source of power and authority for the church to witness effectively to Jesus. Peter's sermon has power because it is earthed in Scripture.

The community of the church is empowered to be so effective, and to see miracles, through its commitment to the teaching of the Word by the apostles and openness to receiving the power of the Holy Spirit.

Each of the above three methods of witnessing worked because it was rooted in relationship with God and each other but also because the believers allowed the Word of God to be reinterpreted by the Holy Spirit (something Jesus challenged the believers about – read John 5:39-40) and created a climate conducive to hear from God the way Paul later described:

I speak the truth in Christ – I am not lying, my conscience confirms it in the Holy Spirit.

Romans 9:1

This effective witness to the Jews of Jerusalem saw the church grow by thousands and become a recognisable (and to the authorities, threatening) faith group. They met both in public places – in the

Collonade (Acts 5:12) and the Temple (Acts 3:1), where their lives were on public display; and also in private homes where they prayed and shared their lives together (Acts 12:12).

As far as we are told whenever they were together they shared their lives, listened to the teaching of the apostles and prayed for one another (Acts 2:42-47; Acts 4:32-37; Acts 12:5 & 12). Not only did they do this as they gathered in homes in private but they continued to live by Kingdom values when they were in public places, showing love and power to the people they encountered and speaking openly about Jesus. Initially, far from this being dangerous, it actually afforded them great respect, and people were attracted by the believers' lives (Acts 2:47).

Essentially this was a church that worked from a defined centre, working its influence from the centre to the edge. People were attracted by the power and presence of the whole, with notable exceptions of individuals who had personal encounters.

We can see this if we look at how healing was released through the church. There are examples of individuals being impacted, such as the beggar healed at the gate called Beautiful (Acts 3:1-11), but there are more stories of healings or miraculous signs happening in larger gatherings (Acts 2:43; Acts 5:15; Acts 6:8). There is even an account of people bringing their sick from all the towns around, further demonstrating the attractional power and community role of the Collected Church (Acts 5:16).

On the whole the church seemed to grow through a mixture of "Mass-conversions" (e.g. Pentecost) as well a gradual build up of individuals ("the Lord added to their number daily" Acts 2:47). This is the exciting potential of the Attractional model.

It is often expressed in larger celebration forms of church and has the opportunity to be a big presence in the community and see dramatic growth. However, there are challenges to be faced, which are also highlighted by the Jerusalem Church.

When Jesus left them in Jerusalem waiting for the Holy Spirit, he challenged them to take the good news not only through Jerusalem, but also to "all Judea, Samaria and the ends of the earth" (Acts 1:8).

Jesus had challenged them directly not only to build on their inheritance, but also to pioneer away from it so that the Kingdom might grow further. As we will look into later, this is a key lesson for us to learn about the contemporary church that is highlighted by the spread of the early church – the requirement not only to understand your inheritance, but also to recognise that building on it can mean pioneering a new form where your inherited values can be indigenously expressed.

In the case of the church in Jerusalem they were given two opportunities for pioneering, both of which initially they missed. The first was to pioneer away from Jerusalem; the second was to pioneer away from being an exclusively 'Jewish' church.

Both of these are summarized in the Acts 1:8 sending, as not only was Jesus sending them geographically away from Jerusalem, but he was sending them into places where Jewish culture was not prominent – for example, Samaria and they were instructed to go to '*all Samaria*', not just *Jewish* Samaria! Jesus had also demonstrated this intent in his lifetime, as he had engaged, for example, with the Samaritan woman and her city.

Again, once the church has been scattered this does happen through Peter's encounter with Cornelius, but to begin with this aspect of the Gospel had been lost. However, the Jerusalem church picks up on neither of these challenges, and it gets to the point where God has to allow a mass persecution to rise up to scatter the church to get them to the places and into the cultures they were called to go into. Even then, as we will see, most of the scattered church still only pioneered away from Jerusalem geographically, and not culturally.

There are only three examples of pioneering from Judaism that we see, which come through Philip (in Samaria and with the Ethiopian), through Peter with Cornelius and then with Antioch.

This is a challenge that we can recognise in modern church culture – for all the benefits and excitement in the corporate community, it is very difficult for Attractional churches to break out of their comfort zones and pioneer away from their traditional forms, while still maintaining their inherited values (we will come to this in chapters four and five).

Yet it can be done, and eventually it is done in Jerusalem. And the way it is done is by the Jerusalem Church seeing itself not as a Centre Church, but as a Minster Church – from which new expressions of church are planted and from which resources and support are sent.

We will see how effective this is when we come back to looking at Antioch, and we will see how the natural order of things is that for an Attractional Church to thrive, it must be prepared to send the pioneers out and to allow Engaged Churches, such as Antioch to come into being.

THE ENGAGED AND EMERGING RECIPES

Next we come to Antioch, which displays features of all three modes but which I would identify is principally being the recipe for the Engaged Church. It is also the first real example of a church plant given in the New Testament. However, we will return to this later and skip on to a brief outline of the churches in Asia Minor and Europe.

These make up the Mobilized Church model in *Diagram A* (page 29), planted out of the church in Antioch by Barnabas, Paul and various other missionaries that travelled with them, and they can be viewed as the biblical recipe for the Emerging Church, as Hirsch and Frost have used the term.

Rather than being started up in a key central place, as both the Jerusalem and Antioch churches were, they are grown in the indigenous places where 'people of peace' (Luke 10:6) are found. They were generally much smaller gatherings of people, and met largely in homes. One of the clearest examples of this can be seen in the starting up of the church in Corinth.

Initially Paul tried to gather a church out of the synagogue – a tactic that had worked in the past. However, finding a distinct lack of peace there he followed Jesus' guidance and left them.

Instead he went to the house next door and found people of peace in Titius Justus (by the name, probably a Roman – not a Jew) and his family, and quickly this church grew … and in the end one of the first and most prominent new believers came to be the ruler of the synagogue that had initially been so abusive about Jesus! (You can read the full account in Acts 18:1-8)

It is also interesting here that Paul is ready to adapt when the "usual" way of going into synagogues doesn't work – another example of continuing the inherited values, but being ready to pioneer the form.

Other churches were set up in Ephesus, Thessalonica, Colosse, and many other places that can be found through the book of Acts and the Epistles (presumably there are likely to have been others as well that are not recorded in the bible). Each of these churches are different, according to their culture and how they were formed. Some are very Jewish in nature, others less so.

The common threads seem to be that in most cases the fellowship is centred around the home, and so we can read that the churches were small gatherings; they are connected by a network of visits and letters to each other and to and from the 'mother church' in Antioch and the Minster Centre in Jerusalem; they are planted with no assumption at all about a Jewish/Gentile divide – this is something that by this point is no longer a part of the Emerging Church's inheritance having been pioneered away from at the Engaged Church level; the new level of pioneering seems to be to pioneer away from a reliance on the 'mother church' and this network of support, and to be more self-sufficient and more spiritually mature – this seems to be a common thread in Paul's letters.

Perhaps the key feature, as with modern day emerging churches in the West, is that they are shaped by the community that accepts Jesus in that place, not by the community that accepted Jesus first in Jerusalem – the emerging churches look completely different to Jerusalem, because they are shaped by a different culture. However, the values remain the same from Jerusalem, through Antioch to Asia Minor and Europe.

In this sense, the three modes of church in *Diagrams A* and *B* are not moulds for the contemporary church. Rather they show an ongoing process of evolution. The Attractional and Engaged churches should always give birth to the emerging but they are responsible for the new church's values, not their form.

You inherit Values and pioneer Form. The Jerusalem Church would not have expected the church in Ephesus to look the same as they do … just to value the same core things: worship, resurrection, prayer, loving one another, and so forth.

As well as seeing the importance of inheriting values and pioneering form, we can also discern how the level of church we are called into can be approached with a biblical strategy. We can see that the Attractional

Church may work best when it sees its identity as being gathered and having the opportunity to operate as a Minster model. The Emerging Church faces the challenge to be mobilized in order to best develop. And the Engaged Church must see itself as being dispersed.

The next few chapters will explore some of the principles that are essential for a Dispersed, Engaged Church to flourish.

Questions to Consider

1. Can you recognise opportunities in your context to become more indigenous to your community?

Notes:

2. Are there areas where you have inherited the form as well as the values where pioneering could happen?

Notes:

3. Are you called to be a part of an Attractional, Engaged or Emerging Church?

Notes:

4. Depending on your above answer, does your church community work to a Collected, Dispersed or Mobilized Church?

Notes:

LESSONS FROM ANTIOCH

4

INHERIT THE VALUES

Before we look in more detail at some of the key lessons we can learn from the Dispersed model of church to be found in Antioch, we must first consider what the church in Antioch looked like. Over the next few chapters we will do this by considering the values, form and vision of the church.

INHERITED VALUES

As I mentioned earlier when thinking about the church in Jerusalem, throughout his ministry Jesus had modelled what would become an essential element of the ongoing success of the church: that of knowing the values that make up your inheritance and pioneering the form that came with it.

We saw how this worked from Jesus to the Jerusalem church (pioneering away from Jewish practices for the sake of keeping in step with God's plan), and also how it worked for the church plants that emerged from the Antioch-sent missionary journeys of Barnabas and Paul (with meeting places, meeting styles, specific local rituals all being pioneered on an inheritance of sharing God's love to the ends of the earth). In each case the values were adopted as central to the new expression of the early church but the expression itself looked different, tailored to the culture in which it grew.

Jesus led a community of faith that preached and practised putting Father God above all else, loving one another and sharing that love – God's love – with the world at large, including extending the power of the Kingdom whenever it would further the cause of reconnecting God with his lost sheep. These were the core values, specifically identified by Jesus across two occasions:

"Teacher, which is the greatest commandment in the Law?" Jesus replied: "Love the Lord your God with all your heart and with all your soul and with all your mind. This is the first and greatest commandment. And the second is like it: Love your neighbour as yourself."

Matthew 22:36-39

A new command I give you: Love one another. As I have loved you, so you must love one another.

John 13:34

For three years Jesus grew a community of faith around him that expressed these values on the move, taking God's word and power with them as they extended the Kingdom by covering the miles. Then, after his resurrection and Pentecost, when the new church was first growing in Jerusalem, the expression changed – no longer itinerant but anchored in the great city, growing at least as large, if not even larger than

Jesus' following at its highest – and yet the values are clearly the same. Still loving God, loving one another and loving their neighbours. By the time we reach Barnabas and Paul's missionary journeys the expression is different again: itinerant mission teams planting smaller locally-centred, home-based, communities. But again, it is the same three core values at work.

And as we would therefore expect, we can also clearly see the same principles emerging in Antioch, and can even identify three dominant values that were inherited from the church in Jerusalem and pioneered into an Antioch expression:

1. DISCERNMENT

The Church in Antioch was firmly focused on being Spirit-filled. When Barnabas arrives – "a good man, full of the Holy Spirit and faith" (Acts 11:24) – they are quick to welcome him and respond readily to the ministry he brings, leading to rapid growth of the community. We can see this too from how they respond to the prophecy brought by Agabus (Acts 11:27-30), or how they know the time is right to send Barnabas and Saul out on their missionary calling (Acts 13:1-3). Always they were sensitive to the Holy Spirit's power and leading and the specific focus of this Spirit-filled church seems to be on the discernment of God's direction. They take time to listen to the guidance of their "Counsellor, the Holy Spirit" (John 14:26).

They were aware of themselves being a church that reached out beyond itself, and to do this they needed to discern where God was opening the doors. Consequently there appears to be a high priority given to having prophetic leaders – Barnabas and Saul have gathered teachers and prophets as their core team (Acts 13:1) and the implication is that they met regularly to listen to the leading of the Spirit.

This Spirit-filled identity is something we clearly see as inherited from Jerusalem. From Pentecost onwards the Holy Spirit is the defining characteristic of the church.

However, in Jerusalem it is primarily worked out through the miraculous. In Antioch, though surely the miraculous would have been present, there is a sense in which the central focus has been pioneered into listening to God's direction for movement ... something which the church in Jerusalem perhaps was not so strong on (hence the need for a scattering persecution).

2. DISCIPLESHIP

Secondly, as with the church in Jerusalem, discipleship was fundamental. This was one of the core values inherited from Jesus as he pioneered Judaism – learning from Jesus how to follow God and live for him, and helping others to learn the same. Jesus had raised disciples (literally, "learners") and in one of his final meetings with them, had instructed them to do the same:

Therefore go and make disciples of all nations.

Matthew 28:19

In Jerusalem there is straight away a sense that others are being raised through the church (Matthias, Acts 1:12-26; Barnabas, Acts 4:36-37; John Mark, Acts 12:25) and that the church as a whole is learning more about Jesus and living in the power of the Spirit (Pentecost, Acts 2:1-41; the fellowship in action, Acts 2:42-47). This discipleship value is carried over into Antioch, and is a major part of their inheritance that they really build on. In Acts 11-13 we can see several examples of discipleship being a priority in Antioch:

- Barnabas brings Saul alongside him and raises him as a leader

- John Mark is then brought in as Saul steps out more into his calling as a missionary church planter

- The very fact that the believers in Antioch were identified as Christians for the first time is very significant, as it shows that their characters and lives were being so transformed by Jesus that their lives were a dramatic witness (the word Christian means "Little Christ")

- Barnabas and Saul have gathered a team of prophets and teachers by Acts 13, who it is fair to read have also been discipled and raised by them, as there seem to be no other coherent leaders when Barnabas arrives, and yet by the time of his and Saul's sending there are leaders in place that are so mature in their faith that Barnabas and Saul can afford to be sent to their next pioneering work.

Surely the Holy Spirit waited until the right time to do this: until the leaders Barnabas and Saul had invested in were ready to take a lead and grow the work that they had begun.

3. DIVERSITY

Then thirdly we come to the diversity of the Antioch community. This is one of the key areas where Antioch knew their inheritance, and did build on it, but primarily pioneered away from it. This creeps over into the next chapter on 'Pioneer the Form,' and we will address this again there, since harnessing the diversity of the church was a primary pioneering function of the church in Antioch that forever shaped the Christian world.

However, the form would never have arrived if the value had not first been in place. The value that the church in Antioch had inherited was one of being open in the community, living out the Kingdom of God in power and fellowship and speaking out about Jesus to all that they came into contact with.

This largely meant two groups of people (as being every day Jewish men and women they were naturally a part of only two communities), those being their immediate community (local friends, families, work colleagues and synagogue), and the religious authorities (Temple priests, Sanhedrin, Pharisees).

They would of course have been surrounded by a variety of other people, but they would not naturally have related to them, and though this does not mean that the church did not on occasion impact these people (indeed, the church's very presence alone had an impact on many as their lives were on public display), yet these 'fringe' people would not have been a part of the core group to whom the church felt called to take the Gospel message. So there was a limited diversity, but this was mainly expressed in a Jewish context.

This is understandable as, excepting one or two occasions, the inheritance Jesus had passed down was a church for and to the Jews. Jesus himself had inherited a Jewish faith and culture, and always stood on that inheritance. However, he then pioneered from it in areas such as the knowledge of God as a loving Father, the immediacy of the Kingdom in our lives, and a life based on love before law.

He did hint at a church for all, including Gentiles (woman at the well – John 4:1-26; healing the centurion's servant – Matthew 8:5-13; parable of the good Samaritan – Luke 10:25-37), but it wasn't until his commissioning of the church in Matthew 28:19-20 and Acts 1:8 that he made the next step of pioneering very clear.

As I have mentioned earlier, this is a level of pioneering that was missed in the early Jerusalem church. They do catch up, largely thanks to Peter's vision and the ensuing encounter with Cornelius, but initially it is left to a scattering of the church to ensure the necessary diversity for their part in God's mission.

As soon as this happens we begin to see the diversity growing, with individuals such as Philip reaching new cultures (first Samaria, then the Ethiopian, and then onto the Roman culture of Caesarea). But it is in Antioch that for the first time we see an cross-cultural diverse expression of church as a core value:

Now those who had been scattered by the persecution in connection with Stephen travelled as far as Phoenicia, Cyprus and Antioch, telling the message only to Jews. Some of them, however, men from Cyprus and Cyrene, went to Antioch and began to speak to Greeks also, telling them the good news about the Lord Jesus.

Acts 11:19-20

As we take a step back and look at the Antioch church we can clearly see this value of "diversity in who they bring the Gospel to" in place. The core value inherited from Jerusalem, of speaking out to the community, has been taken on but pioneered away from its original context as these missionaries redefined what their community was: one based not on religion or race but on a shared city culture, and a shared "under Roman authority" context.

This diversity then spreads and is pioneered further still by the churches planted by Barnabas and Paul, who then reach out to Jews and Gentiles alike - even into Roman communities.

As we have already explained, Antioch itself was a very diverse culture, and so with the church reflecting this in their core values, they were able to be indigenous and powerful in the culture in a new and pioneering way. They became an inter-cultural church, opening the door for the Holy Spirit to use them in any direction, and reach any person or culture.

Diagram C: The three dimensional values of the Antioch church

DISCERNMENT

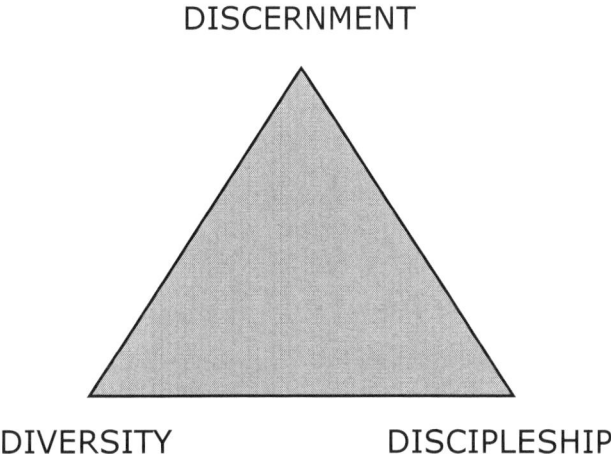

DIVERSITY   DISCIPLESHIP

Above is a diagram of the three relational values of the church in Antioch, based on one of the principles of LifeShapes, a discipleship framework put together by Mike Breen. The triangle is used to help visualise your life according to the three fundamental relationship that make up a disciple of Jesus' life ... "up" to God, "in" to the church and "out" to the world.

In the case of Antioch, their upward relationship was reliant on listening to the Holy Spirit, discerning the Father's will, receiving the forgiveness of Jesus and determining God's plan and calling for their lives. This then became transformative as the church related inwards and allowed God's word to take hold in their lifestyle as they learnt from one another through discipleship. And the power of this discipleship was extended outwards to the world as the diversity of the church grew, directly as a result of their value to include everyone in the loving, freeing Gospel.

I will refer to another LifeShapes principle later on, and hopefully will explain them in passing well enough to make the point and be helpful. However, for further details about LifeShapes, I would encourage you to read either *The Passionate Church* (for leaders) or *The Passionate Life* (for life in general), both by Mike Breen and Walt Kallestad.

QUESTIONS TO CONSIDER

1. What are your core values as a church/church plant?

Notes:

2. Can you recognise a 3 dimensional foundation that God has called you to?

Notes:

3. Do you look to your vision and values to determine your actions, or to your practical limitations?

Notes:

LESSONS FROM ANTIOCH

5

PIONEER THE FORM

As mentioned earlier, a crucial dynamic of the growth of the Kingdom is that it relies on a set of values, first given by God and taken on by the Jews and completed and revealed fully through Jesus, being passed on from generation to generation as an inheritance.

But it also relies on each generation being prepared to pioneer the Form of the church, whilst keeping the values intact. We need only look one or two generations of the early church back from Antioch to see this as a clearly recognised principle, and one that Jesus himself modelled.

Jesus of Nazareth was a Jew. The King of the Jews. He came to complete the Law, and to be the Messiah that was the perfect incarnation of the Father. As such he was fully man and fully God, with his actions, life and attitudes being the absolute model for all we are and do.

As we read through the kind of church he started, though, we get bogged down with cultural differences, expectations that existed then that exist no longer, and vice versa ... so how do we follow in the footsteps of a Messiah who modelled the perfect life in a culture we cannot engage with? Well Jesus had to ask himself that very same question.

He came into the world as the incarnation of God at a time when so much of the life He had laid out had been forgotten. The heart for worship had been lost in the midst of status, power and business; the Father had been distanced from the people of God as one only to be feared so that there was no longer any engagement between the Jews and their creator, other than in their desperation to atone for themselves (a job that God had made quite clear through the Old Testament prophets was not theirs to undertake); the love of God was being drowned by the love of money; the promised life of freedom through God had been diluted by mixing it with paganism and idols that held them captive; and so on and so on.

This was not the world that Jesus had witnessed the creation of, and yet here he was at this point in time to not only bring salvation but to lead the way into a life following the Father into the Kingdom this side of heaven.

Throughout his lifetime Jesus never ceases to be Jewish. He does not start a new religion, or suggest that the Jewish laws and traditions are wrong ... quite the opposite. Jesus lived his whole life pointing to the very heart of the Jewish law, and revealing God the Father in it. He called the world back to a place where relationship with God was the leading beat of life.

He brought a testimony of love from the Father and demonstrated this with the power of the Holy Spirit.

Throughout his life and ministry Jesus did nothing but stand on the values He had inherited. They had not changed since the creation of the world.

However, he did pioneer the Form of the life he was inviting people into. He pioneered away from the ritualistic life of the Jewish tradition and into a deeper and more intimate relationship with God that was accessible to all who wanted to live in the Kingdom. This was still a Jewish faith, based on the same values ... but now it looked radically different, more exciting, fluid and with a great sense of adventure and engagement with the living God.

The church was taking a new Form, and this was a great threat to the Jewish authorities. Obviously there are many things going on in the heads of the Pharisees and the Sanhedrin to make them feel threatened by Jesus, rather than welcoming the coming of the Messiah they had so eagerly awaited.

Money, power and false expectations all played their part but we must not miss the importance of the concern over the Form being pioneered. Too often, even today, we assume that the Form of the church is part of our inheritance – something to be protected at all costs – rather than trusting in the values and allowing God to reshape the form.

This was the trap that the Jewish authorities fell into and they saw Jesus as someone trying to change the unchangeable: their inheritance from God ... blasphemy! They had failed to see that the values were still there and that throughout the ages God had always wanted the form to change with each new generation.

One area that Jesus did not address, other than in passing instances, was that this was a church for the Jews. Jesus was quite clear throughout his lifetime that he had come for the Jews (Matthew 15:21-28), that salvation came from the Jews (John 4:22). Consequently he spent nearly all his time investing in Jewish towns and communities and invested personally in the lives of twelve Jewish men.

However, there were instances in his life where he

showed his long term heart for the whole world. He told the woman at the well that a time was coming when they would worship a God that they knew, rather than one they did not know (John 4:21-26); he healed the centurion's servant (Matthew 8:5-13) and deliberately included other people groups in his parables (Luke 10:25-37). However, these were just hints and tasters for his disciples that he would leave behind.

The clearest sign of his heart came with his commission of them. In Matthew 28 and Acts 1:8 Jesus makes it clear that in the next generation of the church, following Jesus, the time has come to pioneer a new form.

That new form is a Gospel and a church for the whole world, including Samaritans, Gentiles, Romans and everyone else. He expects them to continue standing on the same values (making disciples, teaching them to obey my commands, etc. Matthew 28:19-20) but he expects the form to be pioneered.

This is the way that we can follow exactly in Jesus'

example. He laid out the values for us and a pattern of pioneering the form with each new generation. We only need to be ready to look to the pioneers who have a vision to see it done.

So now we come to the church in Jerusalem. We have already talked at length about what this church was like but it is important to note here that they did not take the hint from Jesus; but instead they took on the form as a part of their inheritance.

This was so ingrained that it took the outbreak of persecution to actually get the believers out of Jerusalem (Acts 8:1) and into other cultures and communities.

Even then, the rest of the book of Acts brings us occasional reports of debates and revelation concerning the accessibility of the Gospel for non-Jews. It seems amazing that they should be so unaware of Jesus' clearly given commission to the whole world ... but this is what happens when you take on form as part of your inheritance!

However, eventually they do get the point and begin to pioneer the form. And so we get accounts of the favour God has for this with people such as Philip (and his encounter with the Ethiopian) and stories of people going to Cyprus and other Greek communities. We do not know what happened there but we do know about Antioch.

ANTIOCH

Antioch is the first church we are told about that seems to get it. In the scattering of the church a group of Cypriots and Cyrenians begin preaching the good news to anyone and everyone, including Greeks. The church grows and right from day one the assumption is that this is a Gospel for all, and so the form of the church is reflected in this.

With regard to what we have already seen of the church in Antioch, it is predominantly the *diversity* of the church that is pioneered. This is the major difference in form compared to the church in Jerusalem that has an immediate impact ... so much so that straight away it makes up part of their core values (as we explored in the previous chapter).

This means that the culture of the church, its meeting places, meeting times, language, traditions, priorities and particular aspects of the Gospel they preached, were different to other churches, because they allowed their form to be dictated by their value of diversity, rather than coming in with a set structure and behaviour system, thereby excluding a whole group of people that were open to Jesus.

Diagram D: Pioneer the form

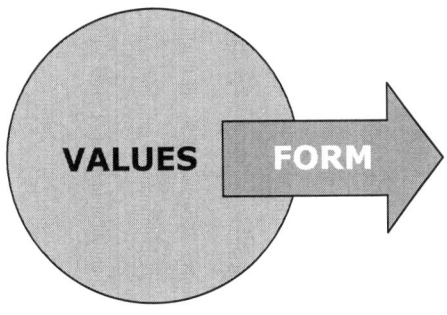

So what was the form of the church that eventually developed in Antioch like, with its new diversity and position in the Roman world? What was its size and influence like? What did they do? There are two main things we can discern from what we read in Acts:

1. A GROWING CHURCH

The church in Antioch, having started from scratch with a few church planters from Jerusalem, Cyprus and Cyrene (modern Libya), quickly became a large church. We know this for a number of reasons:

- We are told that "a great number of people believed and turned to the Lord" (Acts 11:21)

- The church had grown to such a prominence that word of it had reached all the way to Jerusalem, so that the Apostles saw fit to send out Barnabas

- Once Barnabas has begun teaching there, there seems to be another outpouring of growth, and once again the account tells us that "a great number of people were brought to the Lord" (Acts 11:24)

- When Saul joins Barnabas we are told that they "taught great numbers" (Acts 11:26)

- The gift the church was able to bring to Jerusalem was sizeable enough to be worth taking to Jerusalem and be expected to have an impact – even though many of the Antioch citizens would have been poor ... it is reasonable to discern that a great many gifts must have been given.

As the book of Acts goes on the church in Antioch reappears as and when Barnabas and Paul return from their journeys, and we continue to get a sense of its growth and size. For example, after they return following the council at Jerusalem, the bible tells us that, "They and many others taught and preached the word of the Lord" (15:35), indicating that they had by this time needed to build a substantial team to lead this large church.

2. A CHURCH OF THREE SIZES

Antioch was a church that gathered together in whole church celebrations. We know this from the accounts that describe how Barnabas gathered and spoke to all the church (Acts 11:23), how he and Saul taught great numbers (Acts 11:26) and by how when Barnabas and Saul returned from their journeys they would gather the whole church together to encourage them (Acts 14:27).

However, this last verse also indicates that, although they needed to be all gathered together for special events, their day to day expression of church was in fact in smaller gatherings, either in homes or at the least centred in the different sectors of the city.

This would make a reasonable amount of sense as this was a multi-cultural Roman city, as we have already seen, and so the city was built in a compartmentalised fashion with each community having its own quarter of the city (look back to the map of Antioch on page 47).

It is unlikely, though, in this set-up that they would

have met in the synagogues and other public religious places as other churches did, as this was a church made up of many non-Jewish believers. Even the Jewish believers in the Jewish sector of town would have been shunned by their communities for voluntarily worshipping alongside Gentiles.

It is much more likely that these smaller churches met in homes, and quite probably in secret as they had been forced to do in Jerusalem. However, it is also reasonable to assume that in the same way that the Jerusalem church met in homes in secret, but the houses were actually well known to the community, the same would be true in Antioch.

And so we can begin to see a church that not only had a recognisable form that had grown up from the needs of the community but also it would have been a church of some prominence across the city.

The celebration gatherings seem to be reserved for such time as visitors would come and bring encouragements or word from the outside Christian world. The accounts we have in Acts are, of course, Barnabas and Saul but also the prophet Agabus as well as Judas and Silas from Jerusalem.

We can assume therefore that the celebration gatherings would have been great events set aside for praise and thanksgiving and for listening to the word of God for new direction and instruction.

In the smaller groups, then, the church was focused on personal discipleship and living life in community. We can discern this from the fact that this was the first group of believers to become known as Christians (which, as we have already said, means 'little Christs' – Acts 11:26) ... their life was having such an impact on the communities around them that they were being recognised as people who imitated Christ in their lives.

This is not something that could possibly have been recognised unless they were both visible in the community and in a day-to-day context – you simply cannot get that discipleship impression from just meeting for occasional large events.

And we can tell from the references to the growth in the church that the mixture of events proclaiming truth and encouragement and testimony, combined with the evidence of the day-to-day lives of the Christians in their smaller communities, had a marked effect on non-believers and created a culture for the Holy Spirit to move in power and transform people's lives.

There was then a third size of gathering within the church community, which came right from the formation roots – this being mission teams. The church was formed by a small diverse mission team of multinationals, so they would have understood this pioneering dynamic of the church as being fundamental in how to plant churches. So it is no surprise that later we see the missionary journeys being undertaken by a mission team of Barnabas, Saul and John Mark and then later by Paul, accompanied in a pair or team at different times by Silas, Timothy, John Mark (again) and possibly Luke.

This was the church in action right on its edge, and only a small number of people are ever going to be called to operate here, but the fruit of these missionary journeys surely shows us how vital a role it is. And yet so many church leaders feel uncomfortable around their pioneers and don't give them the release they need to form the church in smaller apostolic teams, instead trying to rein them in to "fall in line" with the current programmes of the local church.

Throughout history the church has suffered at the hands of this misunderstanding of the apostolic calling, causing internal conflict and dissatisfaction as God's calling goes unpermitted by leaders who feel threatened by or uncertain of the unknown that these unpredictable pioneers usher in.

So often this has led to splits where there could have been a multiplication of the fruit of the church. Imagine the difference if the 15-16th century reformers had been labelled pioneers instead of blasphemers. Surely the unity of the church would be a much more prominent and powerful feature today.

But I digress! Back to Antioch ...

As we consider these mission teams we identified, it is important to note that while they represent and release the explosiveness of mission on the edge of the community, they are clearly not the only source of outreach in the church in Antioch. In fact the church appears to be growing quite independently of them.

The mission teams existed to push back the outer borders of the church so that it grew and reached new areas and networks. But the rest of the church still had a day-to-day responsibility for evangelism and mission.

As we read the book of Acts it is apparent that Antioch is a growing church, with references to many being saved, but the mission teams (excepting the initial planting team) are not the source of this growth. It may be that this growth is happening largely in the smaller gatherings of the church as the Christian life is lived out – certainly the fact that they were recognised as "Little Christs" by their communities would suggest this.

Or maybe some came because of the impact of the gathered church, as is suggested by the response to

Barnabas' teaching when the whole church is gathered. Either way, the whole church takes responsibility for mission, with each size of gathering being able to reach a different network of people so that the Kingdom can be extended to as many as possible.

Diagram E: The three sizes of Antioch

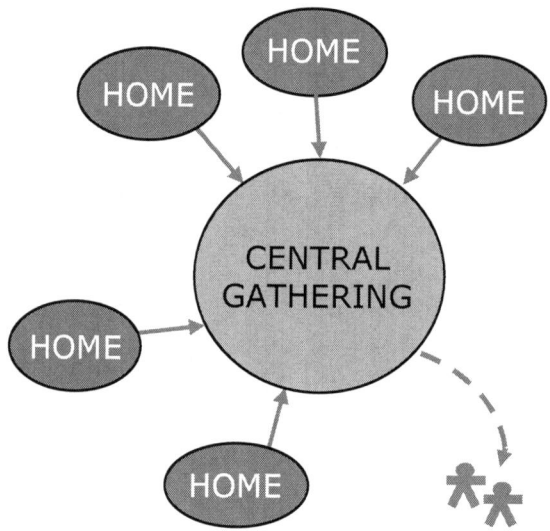

QUESTIONS TO CONSIDER

1. Are there areas of your church that still need to be pioneered to best suit your context?
Notes:

2. Does the whole church take responsibility for mission, or is it carried by the "faithful few"?
Notes:

3. Does the church recognise and look to release the pioneers to start new initiatives and form mission teams?
Notes:

Lessons from Antioch

6

A MISSIONARY RHYTHM

We have now looked in detail at the values and form of the church in Antioch, and begun to consider how their approach to these dynamics might challenge us in our remarkably similar church and mission context today. Over the next three chapters we are going to move on to look closer at the core vision of the church.

As seems to generally be the rule with most successful ventures, a clear sense of vision was crucial to the church in Antioch, as well as to the wider church as a whole. As you read through the accounts of the church through Acts you can see several aims and hopes for where they are going. This is true first as a gathered fellowship in Jerusalem (where areas of vision include personal transformation and healing), through to being a scattered missionary movement in Antioch and beyond.

Obviously we are going to home in on Antioch, and in particular I want to draw out three areas of core vision – the centrality of mission, the importance of developing leadership and a heart for multiplication. Each of these is in the context of the values and form we have already explored.

So let us start in this chapter by looking at how the church in Antioch approached a heart and strategy for mission.

A PLACE TO SEND FROM AND RETURN TO

The church in Antioch was a missionary environment. It was a church started by pioneering missionaries and then grown by an apostolic missionary in Barnabas; and so mission was in its DNA. There was no need for special mission awareness teaching or reminding the church family to look beyond itself … extending the Kingdom of God into new territory was the lifeblood of the church. It really mattered to the whole fellowship.

Specifically, the understanding of mission that the initial leaders of the church (up to Barnabas and Saul) brought with them was one of being built up in faith and then sent out in mission.

This is what happened to the church in Jerusalem with the faith and fellowship built in Acts chapters 1-7, and then sent by being scattered through persecution. It is also what happened for Barnabas as he was discipled by the apostles and then sent out to Antioch. We see it even as Jesus built up his disciples before sending them out.

Consequently it was only natural for the church to expect God to speak about sending leaders away from them for the next phase of the church's spread, so that it was relatively easy to hear when the Holy Spirit did eventually highlight Barnabas and Saul to be sent.

The sense you get with this church gathering is that it is a place *"to send from and return to."*

It's not just that the church was open to the Holy Spirit sending missionaries out from their fellowship, but they then waited for these missionaries to return with news of how God has extended His borders and grown their extended church family.

So we see Acts 13 beginning with Barnabas and Saul being sent out and we read of that amazing first missionary journey and the churches that were planted. But then we reach the end of Acts 14 and we read that once Barnabas and Saul have completed their missionary journey they return to Antioch and spend time giving testimony there and encouraging the church.

They could easily have stayed out with these new churches, investing further in their early development and so leaving them on stronger ground with a greater depth of understanding both of the Gospel and how to lead a fellowship of new faith. Or they could have travelled back to Jerusalem and awaited their next commission. But instead they chose to return to Antioch, to re-engage with the fellowship they had already spent a year investing in.

As we read on we see that this is a natural rhythm that the church engages in: building up the people in the church into greater maturity in Christ and building missionary teams, then sending these missionaries out for them to follow the Holy Spirit in spreading the Gospel, followed by those same missionaries returning at the end of their expedition to help build up the church further on the basis of their testimony and the new revelation they have learned from Jesus.

As we shall see later, this point of returning is also a crucial opportunity for missionaries who have spent a long time travelling and always giving of themselves to spend time abiding in rest, as well as sharing their story, before re-entering the next stage of "people building."

THE MISSION CYCLE

This natural rhythm of build, send, return, abide –
which for the sake of argument here I have called "The
Mission Cycle" (depicted below in *Diagram F*) – is
something we can identify recurring throughout the
story of God's people. The same rhythm can be found
repeatedly in the life of Jesus, in the later ministry of
Paul as well as in the Old Testament. However, for the
purposes of this book we are going to limit ourselves to
the experiences of Barnabas and Paul as we examine
more closely how this Mission Cycle works.

Diagram F: The Mission Cycle

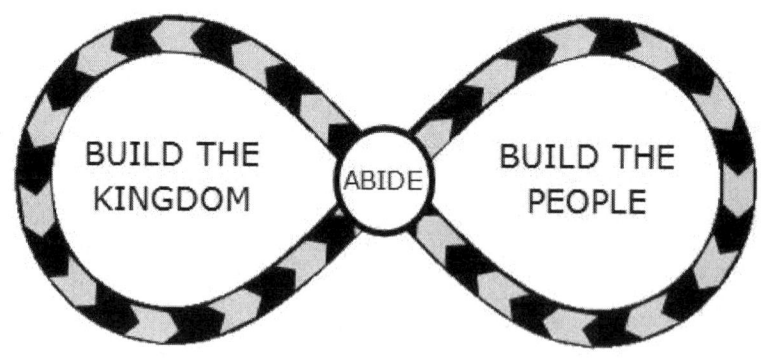

It begins with time, focus and energy being given to building the people within the church. In Antioch this begins (as far as the biblical account shows us) with the arrival of Barnabas from Jerusalem. In this time Barnabas delivers teaching and encouragement that invests in the people already in the church. As this teaching is taken on, and people take what they are learning into their smaller house groups and live it out, non-believers are impacted by the power of the testimony of their lives and the church grows massively.

Then, as the church increases and the momentum builds, Barnabas invites Saul to come and help him. Not only does this spread the load for Barnabas but primarily it means that Saul is discipled whilst being in a place to live out what he is learning from Barnabas. We shall return to look closer at this dynamic in the next chapter on Raising Leaders.

This is the beginning of the team building process. In this case there are two teams to build: firstly a team of overseers for the church who can take over from

Barnabas. This must already have been in place to a degree from the original church planters, and we definitely see it in place by the time Saul and Barnabas are called away, as we see the team with the authority to send them are in a discipling, prayerful relationship with Barnabas.

This is the beginning of Acts 13, and it seems clear that they form the core of a team of leaders already doing a lot of the work. Interestingly, each of the leaders we are told excels in prophecy and teaching ... two of the primary gifts of Barnabas and Saul who discipled them (more on this later).

Diagram G: Building the people in Antioch

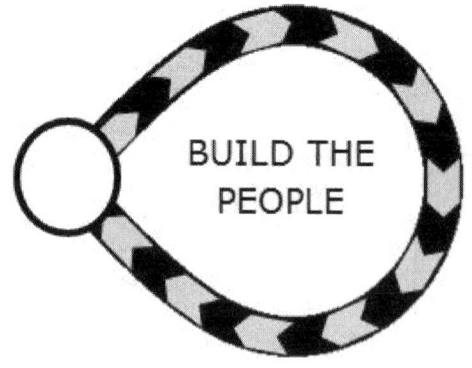

- Barnabas encourages and teaches the church
- Saul is discipled
- Antioch leadership team formed
- John Mark brought in – mission team formed

The second team to build is the missionary team that will be sent out. In this first instance, John Mark is taken on from Jerusalem and after a short time in Antioch being discipled by Barnabas and Saul, the end of the first "People Building" season comes and it is time for Barnabas to lead his team away from Antioch and into a season of "Kingdom Building."

Diagram H: Building the Kingdom through Antioch

- First Missionary journey
- Many churches planted
- Return to Antioch to give testimony
- Time of "abiding"

The following two chapters (Acts 13-14) tell us how this first missionary exploration went. And as we know there are testimonies of success (many people coming to know Jesus, new churches planted, God moving miraculously) and testimonies of difficulty (including conflicts, stonings and the departure of John Mark for reasons unknown), before they finally make their way back home.

Once they had reached Antioch we see that, rather than just taking over where they left off, leading the church and seeing it continue to grow, instead they spend time not working, other than to share their testimony of what God had done.

We know this because of the particular word used to describe them "staying." The Greek word given is *diatribo,* which particularly means a form of staying that is about consumption above other things ... and is often best translated as "abiding"[3].

The testimony they give builds up the church greatly but Barnabas and Saul (now Paul), we are told, just "stay *(abide)* there a long time" (Acts 14:28), with no notable responsibility. This is a crucial time: after a

---

[3] Thayer & Smith, "The New Testament Greek Lexicon", www.studylight.org

season of Kingdom building, Jesus draws his missionaries into a season of abiding, where testimony is the most they have to give. This is in preparation for the next season of building the people.

In this new season we see Barnabas and Paul back in a position of prominence, being the people chosen to represent the church at the important Council of Jerusalem, and when they return they are back into a role of teaching and building the church.

This leads to team building (they are now joined by others in the teaching, showing they have built a team – Acts 15:35), through which John Mark is back in the frame, as is Silas.

Due to a disagreement between Paul and Barnabas they separate, multiplying their work into two streams. Paul takes Silas and they go into another season of "Kingdom Building" (followed by a time of testimony and rest ... read Acts 18:22-23), whilst Barnabas continues his season of "People Building" by taking one-to-one time investing in John Mark.

The next time we hear about Mark he is assisting Paul again, so clearly the time with Barnabas was well spent (highlighting Barnabas as one of the key discipling leaders in the New Testament).

It is worth mentioning that just as with the mission team expression of church we looked at in the last chapter, the "Build the People" stage is not an excuse to avoid day-to-day evangelism and mission. The mission cycle is a natural rhythm of intentional sending that the church engages in on top of the everyday reaching out that is already happening.

Also, the "Build the Kingdom" stage is not an excuse to lessen the focus on discipleship. Saul continues to be raised as a leader and discipled through the missionary journey – in fact, it is a crucial aspect of it. It is about how you follow God's leading and focus (in seasons) on one in order to see both happen.

This mission cycle forms an ongoing rhythm, which can be seen in the lives of all the biblical leaders through the Old and New Testaments, suggesting that it is a rhythm well worth being on board with. Try reading through Jesus' life and seeing if you can see the Mission Cycle at work in his ministry. The result for Antioch was a clear understanding of what it meant to be a church where missionaries were built up, equipped and released, with the expectation that they would return to give testimony of what they had witnessed.

QUESTIONS TO CONSIDER

1. Is there a natural rhythm for your church/group's missionary vision?

Notes:

2. Could an understanding of the Mission Cycle help?

Notes:

7

RAISING LEADERS

Leadership is an important issue in each of the examples of New Testament church models we have. In Jerusalem it was so important that the church be led right that the first corporate act of the church was to draw lots for a replacement for Judas Iscariot as a core leader. This priority continues in Antioch, and we can particularly see this in three areas.

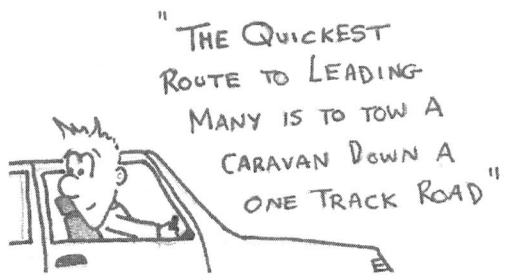

"THE QUICKEST ROUTE TO LEADING MANY IS TO TOW A CARAVAN DOWN A ONE TRACK ROAD"

1. RAISE WITH HUMILITY

Firstly, with the church having been started well by a team of missionaries, and showing many signs of growth, it may have been fair for them to feel that they were doing well by themselves.

However, when Barnabas is sent from Jerusalem they clearly have a sense of embracing the new presence of leadership. Barnabas is not just welcomed as a visitor seeing how things are going, as was his remit from the apostles. Instead he is invited to gather the whole church and teach them.

After a time of this, Barnabas is given further permission to bring Saul alongside him (thereby building a team) to teach and lead the church for a whole year before they are sent off by the Holy Spirit. It seems clear that the Antiochan church were clear about the importance of strong leadership and humble enough to welcome the opportunity to be led by someone external that God had drawn to them – in this case a designated apostle (Acts 14:14).

They then followed his and Saul's leadership and discipleship to the point where not only did the church continue to grow rapidly but the character of the believers led to their now familiar "Little Christs" moniker.

2. RAISE TO REPLACE

The second evidence of a strong leadership vision is the strategy that Barnabas seems to employ with raising leaders in Antioch.

This is something that is never expressly mentioned but clearly it is going on because we get snapshots at different points in Acts where there is obviously a team of leaders that has grown since Barnabas' arrival.

In Acts 13:1 we see a gathering described as being made up of "prophets and teachers." It is a small team of five, including Barnabas and Saul, but they are the people at the head of the church who, not only had a recognised role but also appear to be the people set aside for praying through the direction of the church, and also who have authority to send their leaders into a new missionary venture.

And of course, once Barnabas and Saul were gone it would seem that these were the people that they had raised to take their place and who would lead the church in Antioch from that time on.

As we read on there is no sense that this is a temporary situation – looking after the fort in the leaders' absence. Rather, it looks as though Barnabas and Saul have raised and released this team to do the job fully and permanently.

The two travelling missionary leaders do return to Antioch regularly and they do continue to teach and share encouragement. However, they never resume their role as leaders of the church. That job has been passed on and they are focusing on new ventures (next missionary journey, for example), or on abiding when they are in Antioch.

This way the leadership and reach of the church is spread, with the most experienced always at the edge leading the way and an ever increasing number of leaders, and also initiatives, behind them. This leads to what the book of Acts regularly describes as the "increase and spread" of the gospel:

So the word of God spread. The number of disciples in Jerusalem increased rapidly ...
Acts 6:7

But the word of God continued to increase and spread.
Acts 12:24

The word of the Lord spread through the whole region.
Acts 13:49

In this way the word of the Lord spread widely and grew in power.
Acts 19:20

The individuals named give us some further insights into this team. In the first instance it should be noted that this is a team made up of "prophets and teachers", which are gifts that Barnabas and Saul both demonstrated in their ministry and so we are able to discern that they gathered around them a team of people whom they could disciple in the ways that they themselves had been discipled.

This is a strong leadership strategy ... to raise others who are inclined the same as you and training and releasing them to their potential. In the second instance it is significant where the named leaders came from. Just to remind ourselves:

> In the church at Antioch there were prophets and teachers: Barnabas, Simeon called Niger, Lucius of Cyrene, Manaen (who had been brought up with Herod the tetrarch) and Saul.
>
> **Acts 13:1**

What is significant about this is that we can only account for where three of them came from. Obviously

Barnabas and Saul we know about. The only other one we can discern anything about is Lucius. We are told that he is a Cyrenean, and of course we know that the church in Antioch began as a result of the preaching and reaching out by men from Cyprus and Cyrene.

It is entirely possible that Lucius was one of these Cyreneans who had been there from the very beginning. If so, that would explain to us why he is still a part of the leadership of this church.

However, this may also very well not be the situation. In which case we have to ask ourselves of him, the same as of Simeon and Manaen ... where did they come from? From what we can tell there is no indication that they would have been in the original leading party that arrived in Antioch.

They are not from the right background, nor are they specified earlier, even though by this point they are noteworthy enough to be named. It seems much more likely that these are leaders that have come to know Jesus through the church, and who have been recognised and raised by Barnabas and Saul.

This would be a particularly good leadership strategy in that each of these named leaders represent a different section of the Antiochan community, and so this would form a diverse and expansive leadership team which reflected a community that had grown from a value of diversity, beginning with Barnabas: with his Cypriot heritage (Acts 4:36) he would have fitted in perfectly with the Greek community; and Saul with the Jews.

But then taking over from them there was Lucius with a connection to both the original Cyrenean missionaries, as well as the Jewish community (as Cyrene was a predominantly Jewish city in what is now modern Libya).

There was also Simeon, called Niger. It is not unreasonable speculation to suggest that he may have been a travelling African merchant (Niger means "dark skinned" and this was a central city for trade from all the known world) and in which case he would have been able to associate with the Gentile merchant community, which at the time was substantial.

Then there was Manaen. Although presumably from a Jewish background given his upbringing, he would have crossed boundaries into the Roman community as he was raised with Herod in a wealthy Judeo-Roman context. This would also have given him a great deal of potential political influence and so he would have been a powerful person to have in the fellowship.

The overriding sense you get from this varied team of brothers is that they have been raised into their position from within the church, and have taken to the role with good heart. This reveals to us a vision of training the people in the fellowship, equipping and releasing them into leadership and being ready to send some out into the world as the Spirit directs.

For many churches we can recognise this as a profoundly modern approach to church leadership, and it is very encouraging to see it at work even in the very early days.

3. RAISE IN PHASES

The third place we can look to see evidence for there being a strong vision for leadership in the Antioch church culture can be found in the way that Barnabas took Saul through a discipleship process and then released him into the position of leader, missionary and church planter as we now think of him.

To demonstrate the process of discipleship that Barnabas and Saul went through we will again refer to LifeShapes, as it seems to me to be the most helpful observation of how this process of raising leaders works.

The fourth shape in the series of eight – the square – describes the process of discipleship through the four stages of leadership that Jesus used in his ministry. The apostles then continued to use this process in the early days of the church and so it is definitely worth our while to explore further.

As before, for a full account of the LifeShapes teaching read *The Passionate Church*.

Diagram 1: The four phases of leadership

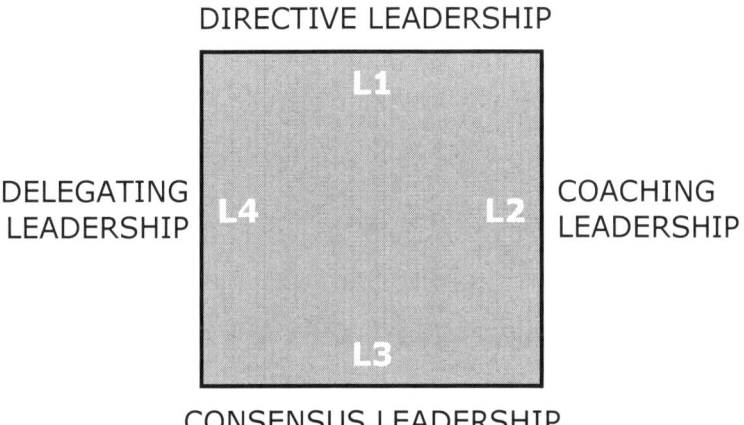

Phase One: Directive Leadership

Just as Jesus begins his leadership of the disciples by being directive ("Come, follow me"), Barnabas does the same with Saul. Although there is clearly some relationship built before Saul is sent to Tarsus, as Barnabas is the one who first recognises Saul's sincerity and faith, the story between these two really begins after Barnabas has seen what is happening in Antioch.

Barnabas sees that his role in Antioch cannot be just as a visitor reporting to Jerusalem. Instead he feels the call to stay and help the church grow, develop and get to a point where they are capable of leading themselves.

As we have already seen, due to the leadership values that are carried at Antioch, Barnabas achieves this. However, the very first part of this process is for Barnabas to bring Saul alongside him – both to help him in his task and also to disciple Saul to the point where he too could become the leader he had the potential to be.

We can see right from the start that Barnabas is the one who can see the potential in Saul – even in just taking him to the disciples in the first place (Acts 9:27). He later follows this up by sending for Saul (who is by now in Tarsus) and bringing him to Antioch.

Throughout the next few chapters of Acts we can see this discipleship relationship grow and develop and there are a few instances and hints in the biblical account to tell us how it is going. One such hint is the order in which Barnabas and Saul are named. In later chapters we begin to see Saul (after he has become known as Paul) being named first. However, in these early days it is always Barnabas first.

We can see that it is Barnabas leading the way, taking the initiative and being seen as the leader. We can only guess what this looked like but it is easy to imagine Barnabas going through a process of bringing Saul alongside him to let Saul see how he does things and gradually bringing him out to a point where Saul is teaching and discipling alongside him.

After a time they are sent to Jerusalem to bring a gift to the church there. Whilst there they take on John Mark as a part of their team and return to Antioch, only for the Holy Spirit to send them (who knows how quickly) out into their first missionary journey.

All through this Barnabas is the first named apostle, and as they set out it is he who takes the lead. By this time Saul has had over a year of being raised into leadership by Barnabas, with Barnabas clearly leading the way and Saul only being mentioned so far as a second string – with no personal accomplishments being mentioned ... this has thus far been reserved only for Barnabas.

Mike Breen has described this stage in a learner's development as being marked by "unconscious incompetence." In this case, Paul is carried by his confidence in his calling and his assurance in Barnabas' experience, not to mention the enthusiasm of setting out on such an awesome vision, all of which shield him from being able to see that he as yet does not have the skills to do the job on his own.

PHASE TWO: COACHING LEADERSHIP

Following the stages of leadership and discipleship round as set out in the LifeShapes square, based on Jesus' ministry, we should next expect a time of difficulty where the people being led begin to realise they are not in quite the exciting place they thought they were – but in fact in a place of hardship, where their skills do not match up to their enthusiasm that has carried them so far.

Mike has referred to this as being marked by "conscious incompetence," where the reality of the shortfall between what Paul can do and what he has been called to do begins to make itself known and the resulting difficulties this causes has the potential to bring crippling discouragement.

In this time the leader changes style to a more coaching role – drawing alongside the team and giving them more time, showing them more closely what they would do, and why they would do it.

This certainly happens with Barnabas and Saul. After a time it becomes clear that Saul must be tested and the opportunity comes very early on in their missionary journey. In the first instance the Holy Spirit inspires Saul to demonstrate the power of the Kingdom against Elymas the sorcerer on Cyprus.

Then they travel to Pisidian Antioch but even though the synagogue leaders there request "a message of encouragement" (Acts 13:15), surely more of a job for Barnabas: the "son of encouragement" (Acts 4:36), it is

Saul (by now called Paul) who stands up and gives his testimony of Jesus.

On the face of things this goes well. However, it brings with it the first persecution of the journey and things begin to get tough. More persecution and the first accounts of stonings follow. This must have felt discouraging ... and Paul must have wondered why this didn't happen when Barnabas led the way.

We do not get too much detail of this but from what we can tell Barnabas' leadership leads to the churches growing (Antioch) and people being encouraged; whereas Paul's leadership so far has produced some fruit ... but a lot of beatings!

Despite this, Barnabas continues to invest in Paul and continues to push him forward into his role, to the extent that by Acts 14 he is now being named ahead of Barnabas in the accounts. We are told very little about the relationship between Barnabas and Paul at this time but this must have been a time of Barnabas encouraging Paul to keep going and to trust that God was at work.

What we do know is that Barnabas continues to teach alongside Paul, as we are told in Acts 14 he does in Iconium, Lystra and Derbe, but increasingly Paul is being given a higher and higher role.

PHASE THREE: CONSENSUS LEADERSHIP

The third stage of the square is when the skills and confidence of the learner begins to grow, and it is at this time that the leader is able to change their style to become more consensus based, looking for their team to be alongside them, taking equal responsibility for both action and direction.

Mike's description is of this stage being defined by the learner's "conscious competence." Paul begins to see the fruit of his actions and grows in confidence. He begins to recognise how his gifts are developing and his character growing, so that God is working increasingly through his ministry. It's not about how good or talented he is – only about how good God is at using his people to further the cause of the Kingdom – but this is a crucial time where God's calling begins to make sense and even be achievable. Teams work more as a team, goals suddenly seem more realistic – there is an "all in it together with Jesus" feeling about the growing success.

In the continuing development of Paul as a leader we see this clearly as they approach Lystra and Derbe. By this time Paul is consistently the one to speak first, is constantly named first and it is to Paul's demonstrations of power that people are gathering ... his competence at being a leader who gathers people and inspires has grown visibly here and for almost the first time he is faced with people responding to his leadership, rather than Barnabas' and his.

It is true that in Lystra this still winds up in painful circumstances as the people take him and Barnabas for gods, and as a result of their defying this he is stoned. However, in the accounts between this and returning to Antioch we see only fruit as Paul's missionary experience at last begins to solidly pay off.

Interestingly it is in Lystra, amongst the heralding of

Barnabas and Paul as gods, that we continue to get an insight into the roles that are held by the two apostles.

Just in case we get the impression that Barnabas has completed his work with Saul and has now become subservient to him by this point, we can clearly see that the definite perception of these two is still that Barnabas is the leader and Paul the one being raised into leadership – albeit with him being the more active.

We can see this by the gods that they are attributed to. It is Barnabas who is seen as Zeus – the king of the gods, with Paul being Hermes – the messenger ... and lesser god to Zeus. This is a fascinating insight as we continue to see Barnabas as the one leading the way but with Paul increasingly preparing to be ready for his own ministry.

PHASE FOUR: DELEGATING LEADERSHIP

By the time stage four is reached the leader, in this case Barnabas, has passed on everything he can and is ready to fully delegate the task, whilst he seeks new vision from God. Mike calls this a time of "unconscious competence", when the learner has learned all he can from the leader and is performing his calling without thinking about it. It has become automatic, though still very much reliant on God, and it is time for the leader to move on.

We can clearly see this happening between Barnabas and Paul. By the end of their first missionary journey it is Paul who is named first, who seems to be recognised as the "leader" of the team. And then, when the time comes for another trip it is Paul who takes the initiative, to the point of refusing to back down about John Mark's involvement. There is a clash of vision here, showing them now to be equal peers and clearly highlighting Paul as now being the thrust for momentum behind the missionary journeys to come.

And so Barnabas takes John Mark back home to Cyprus (both hail from there), whilst Paul takes on Silas and then Luke. And so the work of God is multiplied and Barnabas and Paul both begin a new "square."

The next time we hear of Mark he is assistant to Peter and then co-missionary with Paul again. Obviously, Barnabas was still being valuable for the Kingdom but only because he had the discernment to recognise when to fully release Paul and when to begin the discipleship process again.

This fourth side of the square raises some key lessons for us as we seek to become effective missionaries or church plant/fresh expression leaders, as it highlights the importance of a releasing culture in leadership, where there is such a value of low control that the leader actively expects to work themselves out of a job. It grows leaders who release their teams to take the reins from them without feeling like they are losing control when the team operates as it should and begins to drive more of the momentum, ideas and vision than the leader. Instead, they see this as the time when they can wait on God to take them to the next, even more exciting phase of their walk with Him.

Diagram J: The four phases of leadership between Barnabas and Paul

Barnabas leads the way –
Antioch, Mission trip 1

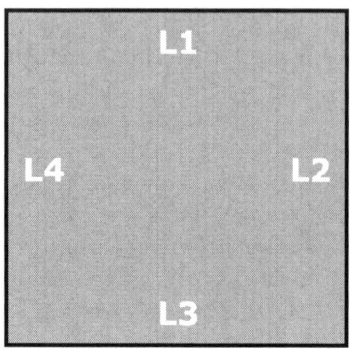

Barnabas hands on to Paul, 2nd mission trip, Barnabas takes on Mark

Saul becomes Paul, increases in leadership (you do, I help); but persecution comes

Barnabas mentioned less... Paul now an equal – appoint leaders together; no persecution... just building churches... fun!

Also, it highlights for us that a "skill drop" is not something to avoid, but something to expect! We often feel reluctant to hand things over to those that we know cannot do the job as well as we can... and yet we forget that the only reason we can do the job so well is our experience, learning from our mistakes and building on our successes.

We have to let our successors go through the same

process, and we have to trust that it is a part of God's plan and rhythm for the work that there be a skill drop. We can see this skill drop happening as Saul takes over from Barnabas and the message is received less readily ... but look at how much was achieved by Paul, and then by Mark, because Barnabas trusted and hoped that they would go further than him.

QUESTIONS TO CONSIDER

1. What phase of leadership are you in with your church/group? Do you need to change your leadership style accordingly?
Notes:

2. Who are you raising to take over and go further than you?
Notes:

3. Do you have a culture of release where people are equipped, trained and commissioned to lead ongoing and new initiatives in the church?
Notes:

8

A CHURCH THAT PLANTS CHURCHES

The church in Antioch had church planting and the spread of the kingdom right at the heart of its identity. After all, it had itself come into being because a group of missionaries had settled there, instead of continuing to travel around spreading the news about Jesus.

As they settled, and as they saw new people coming to know the Lord, it was inevitable that a church was planted. How exciting must it have been to live in an environment where just settling somewhere meant that church growth was inevitable!

It is perhaps no surprise, then, that the church leaders in Antioch were ready to hear the call for further church planting. It was a core value of the church that they should see as many people as possible come to know Jesus and it was clearly a Spirit-filled church environment where God was expected to turn up, where people were keen to hear His guiding voice.

We can see this in the church's response to prophetic words that were brought, such as the word that a famine was coming, leading them not to spend time questioning the word, but to immediately respond in faith by sending Barnabas and Saul to send provisions to Jerusalem to aid their wider Christian family (Acts 11:27-30).

So when the Spirit speaks into a church leaders' meeting and asks that Barnabas and Saul be set aside to be sent away from the church, the church is ready to respond in faith straight away. Certainly it isn't as easy to move from where you are to where you are being sent in the church in the West today!

When Barnabas and Saul then leave it seems

immediately understood that, though they didn't know exactly where they would be going, they did know what they would be doing. We can discern this from the way that the two apostles would pray and listen to God for guidance on where they should go next, but not for what they should be doing (Acts 13:4-5).

The practice of preaching the good news, demonstrating the power of the Gospel and then planting a church from the community of Jesus that grows as a result was a given. It was how they had seen the kingdom spread, and consequently it formed a core part of the values and vision of the church in Antioch. Because they had been birthed this way, they had only ever known this approach to be the natural way the church should be. And so because of this inheritance (again, remember the importance of inheriting the values) the church in Antioch would have naturally understood itself as a church that planted churches. It would have been understood that "the work to which I have called them" (Acts 13:2) was to see the Gospel and the church increase and spread.

So Barnabas and Saul went out as the apostolic edge of the Antioch church and saw the emergence and growth of many plants right across Asia Minor. Cyprus, Pisidian Antioch, Iconium, Lystra, Derbe all emerged from Barnabas and Saul's first journey.

Diagram K: The first missionary journey

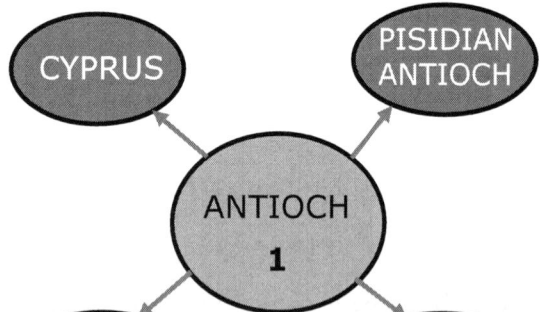

Then Macedonia, Phillipi, Thessalonica, Berea, Athens, Corinth and Ephesus (plus a few others!) were church communities planted in Paul's second journey. It is interesting that the second journey was so much more fruitful than the first in terms of churches planted, and it suggests that not only was it a sign that Paul had now stepped into his life's ministry but also there is greater fruit to be had when the momentum grows for God's work.

Diagram L: The second missionary journey

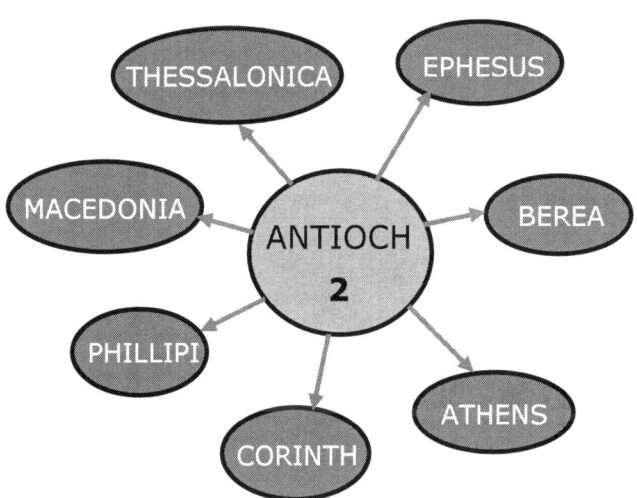

Paul had the wisdom and prophetic sense to know that the momentum of the first journey had not diminished and there was still more work to be done.

His perseverance and heart to spread the gospel, combined with his inherited value for church planting, meant the difference between a blessed time of the Kingdom being proclaimed and the transformation of the known world. It also shows his awareness of his new position as the apostolic leader that he no longer waits for the Antioch church to hear the call but took the initiative himself.

From these journeys the church continued to flourish and spread to the point of becoming the dominant faith in the whole world. Imagine how far we could see the Kingdom spread in our own communities if we shared the same value of multiplication: planting churches and seeing the body of Christ spread, rather than congregating together and waiting for people to be magnetised to us.

QUESTIONS TO CONSIDER

1. Is there an expectation or a hope to continue to look beyond your borders and to continue to plant further churches/groups?

Notes:

2. Or are there ways in which the Kingdom could be extended, and the work of the church developed by applying some of these principles within your current church – planting cells, other services, clusters, etc?

Notes:

LESSONS FROM ANTIOCH

9

WHAT THE PIONEER BRINGS

So we have considered both the values and the vision of the church in Antioch; and in doing so, we have also identified some key aspects of the shape of the community and the subsequent planted communities across Asia Minor and Europe.

Already we have encountered many areas of natural comparison between the world the Antioch church thrived in and our own, and in doing so we cannot escape the implications of challenge, inspiration and opportunity that face us as we read about this ancient church and see so many ways that we could adopt their way of thinking.

However, before we move into summarizing some of the key lessons we can learn in our own context, there are two more areas that we must first consider. In the next chapter we shall look at some of the ways the church in Antioch has already been an influence on the church planting movement in the West. But in this chapter we will address another essential component that is always in place to determine the shape and success of any Kingdom initiative: the gifts and personalities involved.

It seems an obvious point, one that all leadership models would prescribe to today: success is shaped by people not plans. Vision is essential, but it depends on the people with the foresight to see it. Values are indispensable but they rely on the people to live them out. Shape is certainly important to define a community, but it means nothing without people to fill the mould. None of these vital aspects to growing God's church can work without the right people involved.

Now I am not trying to suggest a prescriptive 'right' or 'wrong' leadership personality. Indeed, I'm not trying to imply a leadership personality at all. Any community is only as good as the people are willing to make it, and it relies on total investment from everyone – leaders and participants – who are willing to bring all of who they are to the party. It's not about one personality being better than another to get involved in God's mission. He made us all just as we are and He wants us all involved. But it is about understanding that any community will and should reflect the people who make it happen.

And that does not mean counting some people 'in' or 'out' because "we've already got that gift covered." It is about letting the community be shaped by the people who are attracted into it. But it can also be a case of discerning where gifts are needed and so making sure the sending team has the people it needs to thrive.

This was a factor that was clearly understood right from the beginnings of the early church. We see it in the appointing of Matthias to replace Judas, in the appointing of the Seven to relieve pressure on the Twelve. And we see it clearly in the life of Antioch, from the sending of Barnabas to the inclusion of Paul to the raising of the next generation of prophets and teachers. We could try and examine each of these three examples in turn but I want to concentrate instead on Barnabas.

Paul's contribution is actually more distinct in the missionary journeys and consequent plants rather than in Antioch, and there is too little said about the next generation of leaders for anything that isn't too full of conjecture to help. In Barnabas, however, we have enough material to get an idea of the man and see how his gifts and personality influenced the growth, the shape and the culture of the church, as well as the mission and churches that sprang from it. And in particular we need to consider what has become the signature ministry of Barnabas: that of the encourager.

WHO WAS BARNABAS?

We first hear about Barnabas in Acts 4. It is only a passing mention but one that tells us quite a lot and sets the scene well, so that when he reappears a few chapters later, with his proposing Paul as a trustworthy believer to the Twelve, we are not surprised by his actions.

Joseph, a Levite from Cyprus, whom the apostles called Barnabas (which means son of encouragement), sold a field he owned and brought the money and put it at the apostles feet.

Acts 4:36-37

In fact, we learn from the verse before that this was an occasional practice of many believers. But Luke chose to draw attention to Barnabas in particular as one who did this, presumably because he becomes so significant later on. Luke takes us here through three stages of introduction: his background, his character and his behaviour.

His background is as a Levite, which may by this time no longer mean he was an active servant in the temple, as was his traditional responsibility, but it would almost certainly have afforded him privileges in his synagogue (as is still the case in Orthodox Jewish communities today), so that he was probably very familiar with the Torah and was used to being charged with being publicly responsible for the worship and behaviour of his synagogue community.

We are also told he is a Cypriot, which may explain to us why he chooses Cyprus as his first stopping point on the first missionary journey.

Then we come to his character. This has already been implied by the importance placed on naming him as a Levite – a man of God-given position, but this is not the punch-line. This is a man who so embodies one gift and character trait that his friends change his name accordingly.

Barnabas is an encouraging man. We tend to diminish this a little by broadening it out, saying that his is the best biblical non-Jesus example of a pastoral ministry in the early church. It may well be, but we must remember that in terms of ministry Barnabas is primarily named as an apostle (Acts 14:14), and apostles are not usually first known for their pastoral tact! In fact, I believe that, though he may have been a gifted pastor (in the Ephesians 4:11, five-fold ministry sense), he is independently of this an encourager. I believe encouragement is a gift that can enhance any of the five-fold ministries, and is a much undervalued factor in recognising and releasing people that God is calling.

We see more of his character as we look at his behaviour. He is a man who acts on his convictions, who demonstrates integrity with his life and whose example must have served as a huge encouragement to others around him who wanted to show the same expression of faith through sacrifice.

The reason behind why this short reference to Barnabas is included, is that it informs so much on what emerges in the church in Antioch but more particularly, in the people he serves alongside. And if there is one aspect of his life worth examining more closely, it is his gift of encouragement.

Incidentally, before we move on to devoting the rest of this chapter examining the gift and ministry of encouragement, we ought also to log the observation that it isn't only Barnabas' strengths that shape the communities he invests in. We all have our weaknesses, and Barnabas is no different. For him, we hear in Paul's letter to the Galatians (a church Barnabas helped to start) that Barnabas does suffer from being fearful in the face of Jewish opposition (Galatians 2:13).

It is perhaps no wonder, then, that this is an inherited feature of the Galatian church, as we explored earlier, as they fell into the trap of diluting their Gospel lifestyle by submitting to the heresy of the Judaisers who were intent on not letting go of the confines of salvation by the Law.

THE GIFT OF ENCOURAGEMENT

Encouragement is often used interchangeably with affirmation. Personally I see them as being different. Affirmation is telling someone that they, or something they do or stand for, is inherently good. Encouragement, I think, is more than that. Although it certainly does involve a lot of affirmation, it is affirmation used to an encouraging end: to demonstrate value.

The word 'to encourage', of course, literally means to give courage, to embolden, to spur on, enable someone to stand with confidence where they are. And that's the key word right there: enable. Barnabas enabled the church in Antioch to see the value of what they had achieved and to step more into the promise God had for them. He enabled Paul to become the great missionary leader he was by revealing the value of his calling. He enabled John Mark to recover from a set-back in his missionary life to become the assistant to both Peter and Paul in years to come.

Encouragement was more than a gift for Barnabas. It was at the core of his character – and he was able to live his life in response to the way God had made him, so that encouragement became his ministry as well as his natural inclination.

As a generalisation my observation would be that the church – especially the pioneering church - is quite good at affirmation. We are quick to praise the opportunity-seers, the risk-takers, those who go further than most of us dare. We are eager to be the bearer of good news, the cause of a smile of appreciation, the all-important "someone who understands." And this is vital. But my observation would also be that we are not so good an encouraging those same people – not only saying it is good but being ready and able to prove its value to them, be it with words or actions.

If we want to recognise and release a generation of missionaries, church planters and pioneers to really make a difference then we need to grasp the breadth of encouragement and to recover it as a ministry.

So what does encouragement look like? Let us consider three broad aspects of encouragement in action (not in chronological order) we can draw for ourselves from Barnabas' life:

IT'S THE WORDS WE SPEAK

As I said before, affirmation is a crucial aspect of encouragement, and so our words need to be affirming but realistic. People can tell a hollow compliment and will take it for what it is: well meaning and helpful but short-term but not encouraging. Barnabas knows how to affirm people by highlighting what is genuinely worth affirming:

When he [Barnabas] *arrived and saw the evidence of the grace of God, he was glad and encouraged them ...*

Acts 11: 23

It was the evidence of the grace of God he drew to the attention of the church in Antioch when he first arrived, not the growth of the church or the impressiveness of their church-planting skills. And there is a key phrase right in the middle that makes all the difference: "he was glad." His affirmation is completely genuine. He doesn't fob them off with cheap compliments – "didn't they do well?!" – indeed, he seems not to judge the situation based on personalities or achievements but on how much of God he sees.

But how we use our words is about more than affirmation. There should be a purpose to what we say – not just a purpose for us (i.e. to make them feel better) but also for them (i.e. to step out more in faith). You will have noticed that the last quote from Acts I left incomplete. The full verse is:

When he arrived and saw the evidence of the grace of God, he was glad and encouraged them all to remain true to the Lord with all their hearts.

Acts 11:23

Always there is an end-goal in place. It's not just about making them feel better, or bolder even. It's about making them bolder to do something. To step out in faith, to remain true to the Lord, to not lose heart because of set-backs.

If only we had Barnabas' words to Paul when every new town seemed to precede a new beating. For Paul to have carried on it would have taken more than grit – Barnabas was a necessary companion, his ministry of encouragement vital, and his words must have been extraordinary: proving the value of what Paul was doing and spurring him to carry on despite guaranteed harm.

And people hunger the encouragement of our words. Our own experience testifies to this – indeed, our own desire not only for affirmation but for people to really "get" where we are coming from and to release us into it also testifies to this. It was something Barnabas and Paul encountered themselves. It is only documented once, but must have happened countless times:

Brothers, if you have a message of encouragement to speak to the people, please speak.

Acts 13:15

It happens in a synagogue in Pisidian Antioch, when as far as they are concerned Barnabas and Paul are two Jewish teachers passing through, and it shows what the people were hoping to hear from visiting rabbis. They yearned for encouragement.

Our words can set people free if they are genuine, affirming, purposeful and in response to spiritual hunger.

IT'S THE EXAMPLE WE SET

Acts 4:36 tells us that Barnabas is an encourager and it is immediately followed by a demonstration of it. He is at the forefront to people who sell their land to benefit the rest of the church, which must have been such an encouragement to others around him.

Our actions can be more encouraging than our words, as we prove the value of something by engaging in it ourselves. We show that a person is worth our attention, our time and our investment. Barnabas was a man who, once he had recognised the spiritual value of something, was willing to step out first in order to encourage others to do so.

We see it in selling his field, we see it in the way he invested in individuals such as Paul and John Mark and we see it in his life and character. If we come back to the passage in Acts 11 where Barnabas' encouragement is being described, it is immediately followed by a character statement:

He was glad and encouraged them all to remain true to the Lord with all their hearts. He was a good man, full of the Holy Spirit and faith, and a great number of people were brought to the Lord.

Acts 11:23-24

Luke makes a point of drawing together three strands: firstly that he was encouraging, secondly that this was a result of his character and thirdly that this directly led to many people responding to him and coming to Jesus. His words are given validity by the example he set in his life, and people were encouraged – emboldened, enabled – to begin a relationship with Jesus based on what they saw of Barnabas' own relationship.

This willingness to be encouraging by setting an example is bound to have a considerable impact in discipling relationships, and so it seems to be as we see the difference he makes in the lives of those around him.

Paul is taken from the wilderness to being the leading missionary apostle to the Gentiles. John Mark is taken from being unbearable company for Paul, due to his spiritual immaturity or perhaps his lack of commitment to see the task through, to being Paul's most trusted companion.

Barnabas seems primarily to encourage in this way by accompanying those he is discipling. He sets his example at close quarters, living alongside them and taking on their ministry in order to demonstrate its value and help them to grow into it.

He does this with the Antioch church, coming in as a visitor and yet in response to what they are doing he stays for a year to encourage them by ministering alongside them and helping shape a team of prophets and teachers.

He does it again, and perhaps most notably with Paul. We have already looked at how this relationship developed so we can easily recognise the encouragement that Barnabas' continued presence, throughout the good and the bad times, must have been.

And then again with Mark, he leaves what would have been an exciting life as a prominent apostle to fall into the shadows as he takes Mark away to Cyprus and invests in him personally. The example of humility, of conviction in a person's calling and determination to demonstrate how worthy Mark was of his time, must have had a profound and lifelong impact.

So, being quick to take steps of faith to help others do so, living a life of integrity for all to see and accompanying those who need encouragement are all incredibly powerful forms of encouragement that add strength and authority to our words.

IT'S THE CONFIDENCE WE SHOW

It's about the words we say, the example we set and thirdly, it's about the confidence we show in people. The more we are personally willing to invest in others, the more the value of who they are and what they stand for is apparent. There is nothing so encouraging as someone taking risks to their own reputation, status, wallet or well-being because of their confidence in you to justify their risk.

Much of what we have explored in regard to setting an example could also apply here, but for the best example we have, we need look no further than Barnabas' early support of Paul. Had it not been for Barnabas, Paul would never have even been accepted as a genuine believer by the twelve, let alone licensed to the role of apostle to the Gentiles:

When he [Saul] came to Jerusalem, he tried to join the disciples, but they were all afraid of him, not believing that he really was a disciple. But Barnabas took him and brought him to the apostles. He told them how Saul on his journey had seen the Lord and that the Lord had spoken to him, and how in Damascus he had preached fearlessly in the name of Jesus. So Saul stayed with them and moved about freely in Jerusalem, speaking boldly in the name of the Lord.

Acts 9:26-28

Barnabas risked credibility and probably his status by backing Saul up before the apostles. But he had dared to do something that no-one else had – he had listened to Saul's story and dared to believe him. On believing him, he really had no choice but to back him and he was prepared to do this since he could see the potential in this zealous new believer.

Saul must have felt so empowered by his acceptance as a result of Barnabas' confidence. Indeed, he immediately gets stuck in to preaching throughout

Jerusalem as he had done in Damascus – his ministry has been validated by Barnabas' support, when without it, it could so easily have been different. Had Barnabas not chosen to believe him and spotted the potential then the discouragement he must have felt at the hands of his new brothers wanting nothing to do with him could well have terminally crippled his young ministry.

As if this early encounter were not significant enough, Barnabas shows even more confidence in Saul when he brings him to Antioch. Saul would have realised that Barnabas had seen the scale of the task and known he needed expert help, and from the whole world church he had chosen him – a man who had been sent to a far-away island by the Twelve to keep out of trouble. And then Barnabas does it again throughout their first missionary journey, releasing Saul (now Paul) to be the main speaker – the "front man" of the mission.

Time and again Barnabas shows his confidence in Saul, shows his confidence in John Mark and in the Antioch church. And the fruit that is borne in the lives of those he encourages has eternal consequences. He stands behind some of the most powerful ministries in the history of God's people, content to usher them forwards into their potential with words, actions and reliance. Now that's encouragement!

THREE COMPONENTS OF AN ENCOURAGER

The keys to Barnabas' success are also really simple - not easy, but simple - and can be summed up in three quick observations.

Firstly, he is humble. His purpose is to see others go further than him to serve a God who is higher than him, and his reward is the furtherance of God's Kingdom, not his own standing. Secondly, he sees the value in people. He understands that everyone has their own gifts and ministries and looks beyond personality to the faith and the character behind it. And thirdly, he looks for the good and for God in people.

Barnabas was such an encouraging man because he made a point of always looking for where God was at work. Whenever he saw fruit he looked for the source of it, not stopping until he found it, even in unexpected places. And it will so often be found in unexpected places. Paul and John Mark both prove this! Then, armed with the assurance that God was at work, he could have the Godly assurance to choose his words, to set an example and to show confidence so that those he encouraged truly did receive the courage to step into the calling God had for them.

Encouragement is a choice as much as a gift – it must be deliberate and practiced - and it is an essential factor in effectively supporting one another and raising and releasing leaders in the contemporary church. It is still a value we hold but a skill that is largely diminished. But there is a new rise in focus on it in recent years.

In the last twelve months (as of September 2010) I have had several conversations with people from New Wine, from the Order of Mission, from fresh expressions of church and from local churches here in Norfolk, who are using the same language of feeling that God is asking them to identify and release a new ministry of encouragers alongside pioneers. This is not to say that pioneers need not be encouraging. Indeed, the ability and responsibility to encourage is an essential part of being a pioneer. However, I would suggest that too often this aspect is limited by a combination of a misunderstanding of the true nature of encouragement and also a lack of encouraging support behind the pioneers themselves.

What I think we need is a culture of encouragement that infiltrates every aspect of the church, with pioneers and leaders who will encourage those around them, supported by external people who will come in specifically to encourage the pioneers and leaders. This is the ministry of encourager that Barnabas practised, but has been largely lost in the contemporary church.

It seems clear to me that now is the time to recover a full understanding of this valuable gift and see it as more than a component of a pastoral personality but as a ministry in its own right. People are walking around today stifled by the boxes of 'pastor' or 'pioneer' that they are forced to fit into, unable to experience their full kingdom potential because 'encourager' is not a specific role that is recognised in their context. But if we can re-establish this, then imagine the difference it could make, to be able to release these empowering people to raise up and walk alongside the pioneers who will go further for Jesus because of them.

Barnabas encouraged Antioch, which became one of the most significant churches in Christian history. He encouraged Paul, who became one of the most prominent missionaries in Christian history. The fruit of his quiet work echoes in eternity. So the question is, will we learn from Barnabas as we seek to recognise where God is at work, who God is raising up and how God will grow his Kingdom in our context?

QUESTIONS TO CONSIDER

1. Who are the people in your life or ministry that you or others around you could encourage?

Notes:

2. Can you identify ways in which these people could be best encouraged, through words spoken, example set and confidence shown?

Notes:

LESSONS FROM ANTIOCH

10

ANTIOCH AND CHURCH PLANTING

As Anglican Church Planting Initiatives has worked in church planting and with church planters over the years, the example of Antioch has proved to be particularly relevant. As mentioned in the opening chapter, it has helped to shape the theology of church planting, and it has also demonstrated many of the important principles that have helped people to plant healthy churches over the years.

Most of these principles are relevant to the church as a whole, and whether we are called into church planting, fresh expressions of church or into the inherited church the principles that have emerged through church planting are full of helpful insight. Consequently, so many of the lessons we are exploring in this book have come from the church planting movement.

However, there is one principle that has particularly helped in the church planting movement, which is to look at how the "mother" and "daughter" churches relate to one another. As we have already explored, Antioch is one of the clearest examples of church planting, and of a church plant that in turn plants churches, that the Bible offers us.

As such it gives us a vital insight into how both the "mother church" (be it Jerusalem or Antioch) and the "daughter church" (be it Antioch or the Asia Minor /Europe plants) interact.

Bob and Mary Hopkins, leaders of Anglican Church Planting Initiatives, have used the passages that describe the Antioch community and their church activity (mainly between Acts 11-15) many times in training sessions looking precisely at this issue. This has thrown up many ideas and has led to the development of the following series of observations about how the "mother" and "daughter" churches can bless one another and work together, based on the biblical example.

As suggestions have emerged from this exercise, this has also sparked other ideas that are not expressly mentioned in relation to Antioch but are still excellent principles for the relationship between "mother" and "daughter" churches and so I have outlined them here as well, in the hope they are helpful. Where this is the case, they are included without references.

These principles have all been tested in the fires of experience, and Anglican Church Planting Initiatives has been privileged over the years to see these insights from Antioch be tremendously helpful in contemporary church planting. Many of these are mentioned and explained further elsewhere in this book but it is useful to see them gathered here as they have emerged in this context and been taught regularly over the years.

However, please don't be tempted into skipping this chapter if you are not in a church planting context yourself. For one thing, you never know – God may one day call you into a church planting situation. For another, it is always helpful to have an overview of what is happening and what has been helpful in other areas of the Body of Christ.

But also it may be that there are principles here that stand out to you and that you can see how they might have a positive impact in your own mission or church context in a way that maybe wouldn't stand out when presented in a less training-oriented style.

It may be that many of these principles apply to your context but that the language of church planting – in particular the "mother and daughter" language – is unhelpful to your application. In the rural networked context of my church in Norfolk it is certainly the case that we think less of a sending church and a sent church plant, but more in terms of a network family of community hubs, connected by a shared DNA of vision and values, and we would express many of the following principles differently, or would reinterpret them to fit our particular context.

I have retained the original language of these principles to honour and hold true to the church planting movement they have emerged from, but I would encourage you to ask the same questions of language and applicability to your own situation as we have in Norfolk, so that these essential principles, learned in the fires of pioneering experience, which continue to be relevant, are not lost because of our current perspective of our changing landscape.

WHAT THE PLANTING CHURCH MAY CONTRIBUTE

The following are some of the things that the "mother" church can contribute to the "daughter" through the planting process. The biblical references to where each contribution is expressed in Antioch are included where appropriate:

Best People

The "mother" church can have a big influence on the team that is formed to plant any "daughter" church or mission initiative. As well as releasing those with the heart and vision for the focus community, the "mother" church can look to release some of its best people to the planting team.

This can be a tremendous sacrifice to let go of the people best qualified to lead ministries and initiatives at the "mother" church but it is an excellent way to open new opportunities for emerging leaders and also to give essential support and value to the "daughter" church by investing their best resources.

This is something we will return to again in chapter ten. Relevant biblical passages to read for this include Acts 11:22, Acts 11:25-6 and Acts 12:25.

Wisdom, Oversight and Accountability

The "mother" church is likely to be a community with a variety of experience and understanding, both in living the Christian life and in leading ministries and new initiatives in the church. There may even be a wealth of experience in church planting or mission involvement.

With all this available it means that there is valuable wisdom, oversight and accountability that can be provided. These are so important in order to best equip the church planting team both in terms of giving them advice and help with the planting process, as well as holding the team accountable for their progress and helping them to process how to move forwards. Relevant passages include Acts 11:22; Acts 15.

Intercessors

Prayer is essential right through the church pioneering process and so one of the most valuable things that the "mother" can contribute to the "daughter" is to have intercessors from the "mother" church getting behind the project and seeking God for breakthrough. This not only blesses the planting project but it also cements the relationship and identity that is shared between the "mother" and "daughter" congregations. For a biblical precedent in Antioch read Acts 11:22, 27.

Practical Help

In addition to the spiritual and community based blessings that the "mother" can contribute, there are also some important practical ways that the "mother" can contribute. This practical help might include both financial and administrative support, though probably only for a period until the plant is ready to take these roles on themselves. There may also be other practical support that can be provided, such as loan of equipment.

Encouragement

Encouragement, based on personal knowledge and good communication, can be really powerful and can make a real difference to the confidence and commitment of the planting team. The "mother" church is in an ideal position to offer this (Acts 11:23-24).

Freedom

It can be tempting for the "mother" church to expect any church plant to become a smaller version of itself. However, this can be an unhelpful pressure to put on the planting team. It can also restrict the fruit that could otherwise come if the church plant is able to think outside the box about how it can effectively relate to the community they are a part of. Freedom to be different is therefore a real blessing that the "mother" church can impart. We see this in Antioch in Acts 11:20. Also freedom to experiment and fail, as well as freedom from heavy expectations (Acts 11:23b).

Apostolic Teams

Another opportunity that arises from the strong people resources that the "mother" church has is that they can contribute short-term, servant-hearted, apostolic teams.

The same happened in Antioch with Barnabas being sent from Jerusalem (Acts 11:27-28). These teams may be focused on a particular ministry need (prayer, mission project, etc), or may be focused on spiritual breakthroughs.

Celebration Events

The "mother" church is in an excellent position to provide celebration level events for the two fellowships to share in. Large scale events can be so demanding of energy and resources – including mature gifts of teaching, etc that they are often out of reach for small teams and church plants.

The "mother" church offering these resources helps the two churches remain united and also helps the "mother" church be integrally involved in the church plant project. For how this worked in Antioch, read Acts 11:26 and Acts 15:30-35.

Wider Church

The "mother" can offer a vital link to the wider church family, be that in or out of any one denomination or stream. Without this the "daughter" church can be easily isolated, whereas a link to the wider church offers them a sense of being a part of a wider missionary movement of God as well as providing access to accountability and awareness of what God is doing elsewhere. In Antioch, this comes through the link to Jerusalem that Barnabas and Saul brought with them.

Protection

Finally, protection from error and from pressure groups is something that the "mother" can contribute to the "daughter" that can make all the difference – giving the team and the new fellowship that little bit of space and freedom to experiment and learn lessons in their early development. Again, for how this was relevant to Antioch, read Acts 15.

WHAT THE PLANTED CHURCH MAY CONTRIBUTE

The relationship between the "mother" church and the "daughter" church plant/team is a two-way exchange of blessing, time, influence and resources. Here are some of the ways that the "daughter" or planted church/team can contribute to the relationship:

Accountability

As we have already explored accountability and oversight are some of the key things that the "mother" church can contribute to the relationship between planting church and planted church.

However, this only works if it is two way dialogue and it is essential that the "daughter" church welcomes the accountability and oversight that is offered. There is a clear example of this in Antioch in Acts 15, when the "daughter" church in Antioch welcomes the oversight of the planting church of Jerusalem over the issue of circumcision.

Feedback

The "daughter" church needs to ensure that there is good feedback communications to the wider church and back to the "mother."

This is important as it not only maintains the relationship between the churches, it also demonstrates that the "daughter" still values and respects their relationship with the "mother." Read about the sending of Barnabas and Paul to the council of Jerusalem for how this worked in Antioch (Acts 15:2-4).

Evangelistic Zeal

The church plant can be a catalyst to the "mother" to renew/restore evangelistic zeal and cutting edge mission. Good church planting arises out of a heart for mission or for a particular community. Therefore the planted church should be actively involved in mission and evangelism and is likely to be learning important lessons and experiencing exciting results from their evangelistic commitment.

This can often be an essential example for the "mother" church, who may have sent out all their evangelistically minded people into the church plant. The example of the steps of faith taken by the plant, and the testimonies of their experience, can be a healthy reminder of God's call for us all to evangelism, whatever our church context. To get a feel of how this worked in Antioch read Acts 11:20, 24.

Tithing

Tithes (and offerings) can be contributed to the "mother" church until appropriate independence is developed. And even then they should remain open to generosity and to maintaining their financial commitment to the church that released them and first resourced them.

This ongoing commitment is particularly relevant if the "mother" church has provided, or continues to provide resources or practical help. However, it is also important more generally as another way of demonstrating the value of the relationship. The church in Antioch was committed to tithes and offerings and we particularly see this as they send gifts to aid the famine in other areas of the church. Read about this in Acts 11:29-30.

Sacrificial Lifestyle

As well as being a catalyst for evangelistic zeal, the plant can also be a stimulus and example to a more sacrificial lifestyle.

Church plants are generally small, with fewer resources and less money. They have to learn how to follow their call with less and this can teach planting communities to be more sacrificial with their time, their money, their resources and their lifestyle. Living out the Gospel in a sacrificial way can lead to powerful testimonies as God is relied on in every area of community and church, and this in turn becomes a powerful testimony to the "mother" church, who may well be spurred on themselves to receive inspiration from the "daughter" as they resource and release them.

Acts 11:23 and 26 demonstrates this in the New Testament church as the testimony of the radical Christian life in Antioch feeds back to Jerusalem and they are so inspired that they send Barnabas to find out more detail of what is happening.

Encouragement

Just as accountability and oversight need to be two way dialogues between the "mother" and "daughter" churches, so to does encouragement. In particular, the "daughter" church is in an excellent position to encourage the "mother" into a radical spirituality and experience of "the battle" to gain ground.

The church plant will look different to the "mother" and because of this they have an opportunity to explore their spirituality and allow an indigenous expression of worship and community to emerge. This can be both a challenge and an encouragement to the "mother" to engage in a similar process.

The church plant may also be more missional and have a sharper experience of spiritual battle. This again can challenge the "mother" to remember that they are in a spiritual battle and can inspire them to engage with this more.

An example from Antioch of their radical spirituality can be seen in the Spirit-led nature of their prayer and openness to God speaking clearly to send out missionaries (Acts 13:1).

QUESTIONS TO CONSIDER

1. Which of these contributions do you see at work in your church planting/fresh expressions context? Which do you recognise could be improved or introduced?

Notes:

2. Are there any other ways that you can think of that the mother and daughter churches/teams can bless one another and work together, based on Antioch or otherwise?

Notes:

11

KEY LESSONS TO LEARN

Up to now we have looked at the make-up of the church in Antioch, as well as some of the ways that the Antioch church and culture was similar to our own, and also to some of the principles and values that the church lived by.

So let us use this insight to look forwards and ask ourselves, what lessons can we learn for our own situations today? You may think of more than I present here, and certainly we all should expect to be impacted by different things as God challenges us about our unique contexts. However, to get us going here are my **Top Ten** lessons we can learn:

BE READY TO LOOK AND LISTEN TO THE SPIRIT

As we have already seen, the fruitfulness of the church in Antioch can be attributed largely to the fact that they were ready to listen to the Holy Spirit. They were responsive to visitors bringing prophetic words, and the leaders held prayer gatherings to wait on the guidance of the Holy Spirit. Because of this the church was able to respond quickly when God called Barnabas and Saul to be sent out (Acts 13:1-3).

But it was looking as well as listening. When Barnabas first arrived in Antioch we are told that he "saw the evidence of the grace of God" (Acts 11:23). He went to Antioch to see what was happening with spiritual eyes, and as such he recognised what God was doing and saw where to join in.

The key lesson here for us is that we need to cultivate a culture of expectation in our fellowships and communities. We need to pray and listen to the prophetic leadings of the Holy Spirit and expect Him to send people out "to the work to which He has called them" (Acts 13:2)

And we should look with the eyes of faith to see the qualities He is developing, in us and those around us, and the openings for the Gospel He is initiating in our context. In short, asking: Lord, where are you at work? This way we are far more likely to see God leading the way into the places and situations that He has prepared. And we will see a greater level of God working in and through our lives.

Of course, for this to take hold in our lives the sacrifice we need to be willing to make is to be flexible to the point of ditching plans and preparations at a moment's notice when we hear God say something new and unexpected (a not uncommon occurrence!). We also need to be ready to listen and look with faith and to have the discipline not to be sceptical when words are shared that are contrary to our hopes and plans! This takes humility before God – the humility to submit our lives to Him in the knowledge that he will use us better than we might otherwise have intended.

We need to hold tightly to our values and loosely to our plans, so that when we take time to listen to God we expect Him to speak and are ready to hear Him, whatever the call.

Notes:

RELEASE THOSE WHO ARE CALLED

In terms of effective leaders, Barnabas and Saul were the most prominent the church in Antioch had. They did the teaching, raised the leaders, stood in the gap between Antioch and Jerusalem and were central to seeing masses of people come to know Jesus and join the church. Were they ever to leave the "skill drop" would have been obvious and yet when the day came for God to call them away, there were no complaints or doubts or fears. We only see a church that was ready and willing to release those who they recognised had been called.

Surely, this is a crucial (and for many of us, painful) principle to take on board, particularly if we are looking to start churches or groups, or send out mission teams. The temptation is overwhelmingly to keep our leaders at the centre of church, presuming that this is the ideal place for them as they can continue to help grow the community at the centre, including raising the new leaders that would then actually start the church or form the mission team. There are times when holding on to our established leaders is precisely the right approach but the challenge of Antioch is to be ready for this not to be the default position.

On the other hand, sometimes the opposite problem emerges, and it is only the existing recognised leaders who are considered for pioneering activity. There are plenty of good reasons for this – they are experienced, they are trained, they are proven to be reliable. But sometimes they are only the "safe option" that may not tally with God's plan.

There may be unsung heroes of faith in our church communities that God has placed "for such a time as this" (as with Ruth) who have so far gone unnoticed, such as the relatively obscure figure (at the time) of John Mark in Antioch. He had not been around for very long, and seems to have no prominent ministry role, and yet the Antiochan elders were just as ready to hear his call as Barnabas and Saul's.

The key in both cases is for the call, and not the competence to be the reason for sending out. We need to listen eagerly for God to speak to us about who He is calling, and into what. We do this by clearly teaching our values, encouraging personal vision and being sensitive to the Spirit's prompting of our hearts, our attention and our circumstances.

We must be ready to ensure that new initiatives and mission endeavours are resourced with the very best they can have, even if that means releasing our most valued or, at the other end of the scale, untested people. In any event the principle is to give quality, and give though it really costs.

Notes:

8

Raise Leaders

We explored how this was an essential part of the church in Antioch in chapter seven, so we have already seen the potential impact that a healthy culture of raising leaders can have. Over the years, in both church growth and church planting/mission circles, it has consistently been recognised as one of the most crucial factors for success.

It is all too easy to rely on the skills and commitment of a few (and usually just the minister and an exclusive "inner circle") but the church in Antioch and the subsequent church plants in Asia Minor and Europe seemed to work more on a principle that the leaders were raised from within. Barnabas and Saul are very notable exceptions, both having been "bussed in", so to speak, but as we have already seen others of the Antioch church leaders appear to have been "home grown." The same is repeatedly the case in the subsequent accounts of Barnabas and Paul's church planting exploits: they gather the community but then leave it in the hands of local Christians. And because of this approach, the potential for God to multiply the work of the church was dramatically widened.

If we want to see similar multiplication of the fruit of God's work in and through us then we need to place a high priority on raising leaders from within, looking for the opportunities to release them into what they are passionate about and teaching them in turn to raise new leaders behind them.

This is one of the basic principles of effective passing on to the next generation. We should all be in the process of following those ahead of us and then leading others to take over from us and go further than we have. Sheep from the front, shepherds from behind!

Notes:

Momentum Builds a Movement

We also mentioned earlier about how Paul recognised after the first missionary journey that the momentum for church planting had not diminished, and that his call in life was to press on with this cause and see the gospel and the church spread through the Gentiles all the way to Rome.

It was this momentum being maintained that really transformed Christianity from being a radical Jewish sect to a whole-world movement. And as a world faith it has never lost that movement in almost two thousand years, even though it is made up of so many areas of the body of Christ that has seemingly lost its original momentum!

There is a line of sociological thought, which I first heard explained to me at a conference of church leaders in Denmark in January 2006 but I believe is quite firmly established, that suggests there are four stages that all institutional entities go through from birth to institution.

Broadly summarised these are that they all start when the work of a man begins to gather *momentum*. As it does so, it draws others alongside who share the same values and hopes and before long it has become a *movement*. The movement continues to grow. However, its success is also what sets in motion the next stage: as the movement requires more attention to keep it going and growing, it becomes a *management*. And then eventually it becomes the victim of its own high-maintenance, setting in place procedures and practices that hold it steady and secure, but also static. For better or worse it has become a *monument* (see *Diagram M* on page 206).

I am not trying to suggest that monuments are exclusively bad, but the sad truth is that so many monuments were birthed in the energy of vision but have become distant from the world that vision had touched. And they wish they still had that same flexibility of old to move and shift according to the needs and shape of the world they now find themselves in, to have that same impact as in their days of momentum.

Diagram M: From momentum to monument

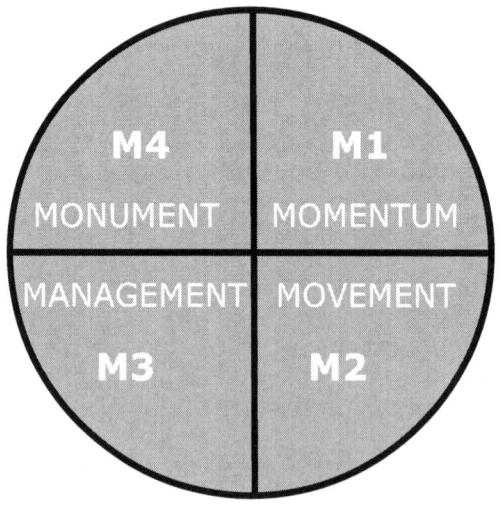

The sociological argument is that this cycle is unavoidable, and certainly the history of the institutional churches would seem to back that up. But if this is so, how has Christianity as a world faith managed to maintain itself primarily as a movement?

For me, the key to this is that, though any one example of momentum from God may eventually become a monument, there is a time during the *movement* stage where the opportunity arises to release the pioneers to create new momentum.

Again, this raises the importance of both raising leaders and releasing your best, but also shows the importance of constantly praying through and observing what stage the church, plant or mission project is at? Are there new leaders coming through, pulling away from the "traditions" we are developing? Can they be released to generate new momentum?

Barnabas goes through this process as he is dissatisfied to continue working with Paul just to revisit the old plants and see them develop (Acts 15:36-41). He can see this approach developing from a movement into a management – just checking up and helping to grow what has now been done. Instead he wants to build on this, using the journey to continue discipling John Mark as a missionary leader.

This jolt seems to prompt Paul, albeit through a

disagreement, to also shift his plans and he extends his mission to going to new places and seeing a new momentum emerge to continue to grow the movement.

It is a final lesson in leadership from Barnabas before they part – one that Paul learns very quickly.

From here on Paul lives his life between missionary journeys, stays in prison and times of abiding back in Antioch. However, he no longer seems to take part in any of the actual leadership of the church in Antioch, which ends up going through its own cycle to become a monument of the early church. Instead, Paul is at the head of the pioneering leaders, constantly looking for the fresh momentum.

This is a key issue for us. We may all be able to think of church plants or groups that grew and developed out of the energy of momentum, then became a movement but now are so successful that they are more managements or even monuments.

As I said, I'm not casting aspersions. Even from a pioneering missional point of view, this need not bad thing. Indeed, the future success of the church depends on having a few permission-giving monuments. Becoming a monument of faith can be a healthy aspiration, so long as they see as part of their remit the responsibility to look for and release the new momentum, which many do.

But we must make sure we are watching and at every stage looking for the new momentum to see the gospel and church spread further.

Notes:

THINK BIG BY ACTING SMALL

It is a small point, but this is an important example that is given to us by the church planting movement which emerges out of Antioch. All the way through the planting of the Antioch church and the missionary journeys, there was a sense of the leaders knowing there was a bigger picture, even having a long-term vision, but always being focused on where they were in the moment.

They really did heed Jesus' words not to worry about tomorrow, and paid attention to the need to "act small". As a result each new church was started with close attention and care, and individuals' lives were transformed.

But at the same time there is also the sense that Barnabas and Saul have a heart to see a mass-scale transformation through the gospel. They know they are on an extensive journey, are expecting God to do amazing things and have a yearning and vision to see God's kingdom spread throughout the Gentile world, with no cultural or geographic boundaries.

We need to make sure we hold on to the overall, big vision God has given us while at the same time not forgetting to "act small" by concentrating our time and energy into the activity of each day.

Notes:

5

Know Your Community

There are numerous occasions where it is clear that having an awareness of the community that you are reaching out to is a high priority.

In a cross-cultural city such as Antioch, it is a multi-cultural team of missionaries that start the church among those of their own background. In Athens, Paul walks in the market square, spends time in their libraries and quotes their poets in order to communicate the Gospel in a way that would connect with his listeners (Acts 17:16-33).

Then later, as he writes to Titus, we see that he must have done the same on Crete as he gives specific knowledge about the Cretans' prophets (Titus 1:12). There are other examples if you look for them, but these alone show that a definite lesson we can learn is the importance of becoming familiar with the community we are called to be a part of.

However we choose to do this – be it a mission audit (see "Additional Resources" at the back of this book), prayer walking, questionnaires, talking to people, gathering what we already know, etc – it is vital that we follow Jesus' call for us to "open your eyes" as we consider the mission field before us (John 4:35). Only then can we have a clear idea of how we can communicate the gospel to the community, and begin to understand what it is that God is calling us into for the next season.

Notes:

INHERIT THE VALUES, PIONEER THE FORM

Again, this is an issue we have explored in greater detail earlier in this book, but it is such an important observation that it is important we include it in our list of top lessons for us today.

We don't need to cover how this was expressed in Antioch again – but do re-read chapters three and four for the detail! – except to reaffirm how essential a factor this was in the explosive growth of the early church.

Because the same values were carried down the family line – to love God, love one another and love your neighbour – there was integrity in the movement; but because of the willingness to pioneer the form according to specific cultures and contexts, it enabled the church to always be a community that invited people to encounter the God that knows them, made them as they are, will relate with them accessibly and set them free.

If we want our churches, plants and mission initiatives to have that same flexibility today then the first step is to recognise and honour the values we have inherited – both the general values of the Gospel and the specific values of the church we have planted out of or are still a part of. This becomes our foundation, and a focal point for where we return to as old things die and new initiatives grow.

However, we must not confuse our values with our form. And we must be ready to pioneer the form in order to see Jesus' values reinterpreted with each new generation so that the church remains the most relevant and spiritually dynamic community to be a part of that it can be.

Notes:

MULTIPLICATION IN MISSION AND DISCIPLESHIP

As we consider what the church in Antioch was like one of the observations we can make time and again is that there is a priority and expectancy given to multiplication.

This emerges as we see how the church was first planted, through the multiplication of the church in Jerusalem; and also in the way that leaders are raised and discipled, by Barnabas or Paul pouring themselves into others and then seeing their teams multiply and spread.

Ultimately, this attitude of multiplying the work of God is the difference between the initial growth in Antioch settling into being an effective city-based church and its giving birth to a dynamic movement of mission across the whole known Gentile world.

The challenge for us today is clear: do we carry that same desire to see expressions of the Kingdom multiply? Are we, and the communities of which we are part, ready we do what it takes to multiply what we have – churches, congregations, cells, leaders, discipleship, mission activity, etc, etc?

I write this as someone who has seen glimpses of what can happen when multiplication is the end-goal of what is started, and it is definitely worth pursuing! But there is a price to pay, and again it comes down to our willingness. In this case, it is our willingness to let go of our comfort zones.

Multiplication is often far more exciting for everyone else than for us, because for us it can involve saying goodbye to valuable people in our fellowship as either they or we set out in a new direction; it can involve leaving something that is fully established and comfortable to start all over again, surrounded by new challenges and that not-missed feeling of never knowing what you're doing; it can involve taking dangerous steps of faith into new places to meet new people, and the courage to talk to them openly about issues of faith; it can involve giving up time, energy, money and all manner of personal sacrifices for initially comparatively little comeback compared to what you have become accustomed to.

And yet, when the new initiative begins to grow and the fruit starts to become apparent, there is nothing else like it – to know that God has used you to further His plans and expand His Kingdom.

It is sufficiently hard that we need to make it an intention right at the beginning, so that when we get there, what it costs is less significant than the opportunity it gives to celebrate what God has already done and look forward to the even greater things to come.

Notes:

2

HAVE CONFIDENCE IN THE GOSPEL

Throughout the planting of the church in Antioch and the Asia Minor/Europe church plants there was a great confidence in both the power of the good news of Jesus, and also in the power of the Kingdom demonstrated through miracles.

Barnabas and Saul are unashamed in preaching the Gospel and naturally see healings, demons cast out and other miracles. This goes beyond their ministry, entering their whole life as they trust God for provision, direction and protection. It gives their faith integrity and authority, and by this faith they see God moving in transforming power in different communities across Asia Minor and Europe. If we shared the same level of confidence in our faith imagine what God could do through us! The Gospel is not out of date and God has not stopped moving in power ... Jesus is the same yesterday, today and forever!

I talked before about how, in terms of miracles, the Gathered Church in Jerusalem can sometimes seem so much more powerful than the Dispersed and Mobilised Churches a few chapters later, but that this is actually not the case. It is just that the whole church is gathered into one condensed place, and the miracles reflect this. The same miracles continue to happen afterwards – indeed, they are more widespread (across the globe) – just not all in the same room!

The same is true today. God is just as active now as ever, and we can have the confidence to expect Him to move among us as we step out in faith.

Notes:

BUILD MISSION INTO THE CULTURE

And finally, for our number one ...

Everything about the church in Antioch was about mission. The purpose of the church, its actions and message, the church plants that grew from there ... they all happened as a result of a high priority of reaching into different communities and different people's lives with the Gospel, wanting nothing less than for everyone to have the opportunity to be in relationship with their loving heavenly Father.

This is what we mean when we talk about mission – it is not about talking about God because "that's what we have to do." It is about living our lives to further God's ultimate salvation plan for His creation and His people. It includes our words, our lifestyles, our relationships, our social (or even political) engagement, our priorities and everything else.

However we inject this, be it through a similar

mission cycle as the one we have explored in chapter six, or by other means, we must have this basic principle of "mission first" at the centre. If we learn nothing else from the church in Antioch, let us learn the need for a mission heart.

Through one church in Antioch God changed the best part of a continent. We may not seek the same level of impact but if our hearts are set on mission then we can begin to step into the "life to the full" that Jesus has called us to (John 10:10) and we can be available to serve Him for the glory of His kingdom, seeing growth, miracles and lives transformed along the way.

Notes:

QUESTIONS TO CONSIDER

1. As you look at your church context, which of these Top 10 lessons have you already engaged with?
Notes:

2. How could you continue to develop these areas?
Notes:

3. Which lessons are you most challenged by and need to build into your church/group's culture?
Notes:

LESSONS FROM ANTIOCH

12

RESPONDING IN FAITH

So what do we do with these lessons from Antioch? We need to respond in faith. If we are in a church planting context then this is as near to a biblical blueprint as we are ever likely to get. But even if we are not, and are just engaging with developing the contemporary church context we find ourselves in (be that whole church, cell or mission team), there is still so much for us to learn and put into action here.

Despite the different time in history and culture, the mission context of Antioch and Asia Minor/Eastern Europe was remarkably similar to the West today, as we have discussed earlier, and there was a definite heart to see the gospel and church increase and spread, with amazing results.

If we want to see similar things happen amongst us today, then why should the lessons that the church in Antioch teaches us not still be relevant today? God has not changed. His power has not diminished. His intent to see the world come under the banner of heaven has not wavered. The gospel is as powerful and relevant today as it was then, and the church continues to be the first and only choice for how God will reach his lost sheep.

I encourage you to recall each stage of this book, as we have uncovered the different layers and lessons from Antioch. Add in any that you yourselves have thought of that I have missed. And ask yourselves:

- How do each of these aspects challenge my mission context?

- How could my part in the body of Christ increase and spread by stepping out in similar ways to the church in Antioch?

If you are in a phase of preparing or building up to a church planting or a mission project, then it may be good to get together with your leading team to consider these things. Or, if you are in any ongoing church situation, then perhaps there are important questions here that can bring new impetus or a fresh vision into what is already happening.

Whatever the situation, the church in Antioch has the potential to be a model for us as we seek to take strides, instead of steps, forward for Jesus and the wider these challenges are thought through, prayed through, discussed and implemented the better.

There is nothing to stop us serving God in the same way today as Barnabas, Paul and the Antioch church leaders all those years ago. Nothing but fear and doubt. They have paved the way ... will we now respond in faith in the same way they did?

QUESTIONS TO CONSIDER

1. How do each of these aspects raised in this book challenge my mission context?
Notes:

2. How could my part in the body of Christ increase and spread by stepping out in similar ways to the church in Antioch?
Notes:

BRIEF BIBLIOGRAPHY

Michael Frost and Alan Hirsch, *The Shaping of Things to Come*, Hendrickson, 2003.

Mike Breen and Walt Kallestad, *The Passionate Church*, Nexgen, 2005.

Mike Breen and Walt Kallestad, *A Passionate Life*, Nexgen, 2005.

Bob Hopkins, *Making Sense of Emerging Church*, ACPI Web-articles (www.acpi.org.uk), 2006.

Bob Hopkins and Mike Breen, *Clusters: Creative Mid-sized Missional Communities*, 3DM, 2008.

Mark Stibbe and Andrew Williams, *Breakout: One Church's Amazing Story of Growth Through Mission-Shaped Communities*, Authentic, 2008.

Phil Potter, *The Challenge of Cell Church: Getting to Grips with Cell Church Values*, BRF, 2001.

Robert D. Dale, *To Dream Again*, Baptist Sunday School Board, 1981.

Linda Tue, *Lessons on Leadership from the Church in Antioch*, Web-article (www.bsop.ph) 2004.

Thayer and Smith, *The New Testament Greek Lexicon* (www.studylight.org).

USEFUL WEBSITES

www.acpi.org.uk

The website for Anglican Church Planting Initiatives. This is an excellent site, with regular articles posted on current issues for church planting and fresh expressions of church. There are also resources to buy and an archive of helpful articles to download.

www.3dministries.com

The central website for 3 Dimensional Ministries – a mission partnership and resources network headed up by Mike Breen. Not only is this an excellent hub for teaching and church pioneering resources, but there are also links to 3dm mission partners involved in Antioch-style church across the world. This is also the best place to start when exploring available LifeShapes material.

www.sacred-destinations.com

An interesting website linked to research done by Princeton University in the USA. It contains information about ancient biblical sites, including an excellent archeological map of ancient Antioch and a wealth of other related information.

www.bibleplaces,com

Similar themed website to above, focusing on the history and culture of ancient biblical places and communities.

ADDITIONAL RESOURCES

Other published works by the same author:

Listening for Mission
Co-written with Steven Croft and Bob Hopkins, Church House Publishing, 2006.

Coaching for Missional Leadership
Co-written with Bob Hopkins ACPI & FE, 2009.

A Pioneer's Understanding of the Church
Co-written with Bob Hopkins, ACPI, 2010.

The Lost Story: The Scroll of Remembrance
Emblem Books, 2010.

Forthcoming titles from Emblem Books:

Where Streams of Living Water Flow by Paul Lewis